INTRODUCTION TO PROJECTIVE COGNITION
A Mathematical Approach

INTRODUCTION TO PROJECTIVE COGNITION
A Mathematical Approach

Luis O. Cruz

Philosophical Library
New York

Library of Congress Cataloging in Publication Data

Cruz, Luis O.
  Introduction to projective cognition.

  Bibliography: p.
  1. Cognition—Mathematical models. I. Title.
BF311.C78   1985   153   83-26278
ISBN 0-8022-2448-2

Published 1986 by Philosophical Library, Inc.
200 West 57th Street, N.Y., N.Y. 10019.
Copyright 1986 by Luis O. Cruz.
All rights reserved.
Manufactured in the United States of America.

Contents

	Introduction	vii
Chapter 1	*Concepts*	1
	Definitions	6
	Vector and Scalar Concepts	8
	The Cognitive Inversion	9
	Vectorial Concepts	12
	Scalar Concepts	15
	Simple Inverse Algebra	19
	Cause and Effect	22
Chapter 2	*Thematic Field Theory*	24
	Mental Operators	27
	Matriceal Cognitive Multiplication	32
	Disconnection	36
	Imaginary Cognitive Inversion	37
	Compound Thematic Fields	39
	Thematic Field Conversion	40
	Reverse Template Matching	41
Chapter 3	*The Inversive Phenomenon*	43
	Knowing as an Inversive Alternative	43

	Graphical Principles of the Inversive Act	47
	Symmetry	50
	Continuity	53
Chapter 4	*Uncertainty*	56
	Quantitative Uncertainty	58
	Qualitative Uncertainty	59
	Disconnected Type of Uncertainty	60
	Hyperbolism	62
Chapter 5	*Memory*	63
	Disconnection	63
	Memory	65
	Backward Masking	68
	Reading	69
Chapter 6	*Time and Space*	72
	Time	72
	Space	77
Chapter 7	*Perception*	82
	Vector and Tensor Phenomenal Theory	85
	The Riemann-Christoffel Tensor	86
	The Cosmological Perceptive Constant	87
	Geometry of the Sphere	89
	Cosmological Perceptive Principles	101
	Symbolic Summary of Chapter Seven	102
	Perceptive Orbital Motion	103
	Appendix	111
	Bibliography	113

Introduction

The act of being aware, or consciousness, is a mental process that goes on in an orderly and systematic way. The functions and attributes of this act are definable by a set of rules not apparent in everyday cognitive happenings; its unchanging ways can be easily delimited and its particular mechanisms can be made amenable to an orderly scientific language. To be conscious of something is to be able to retain the personal self untouched among unique time-space relations that in themselves are neither close, distant, past or future. These rules continuously guide the human experience of cognitive physical and temporal facts. Every conceptual cognition (awareness) undergoes a perceptive *projection* ruled by mental laws that are infallible and constant. The fundamental supposition to be proposed in the following treatise is that these workings of internal personal living have real and finely ruled processes that establish mental mechanisms as well as they define the law and order of the external physical world.

Our first objective is to proceed to establish these mechanisms of internal awareness. In order to do this, the personal self must be allowed to retreat into an *expectant* state of mind, where it will not *protect* the manifestations and consequences of its own strict laws. All experience of personal cognition must be allowed to follow this expectancy condition, even if these experiences convince the Ego in an unmistakenly way that there is no rule. To achieve this, a number of introspections must be set apart and distinguished from another group of personal introspections; the first ones will form a *perceptive* act, not subject to the acceptance by second observers, while the character of the latter ones will be general, to be used as common knowledge available to all observers. Thus, an important objective of this treatise is the formation and description of psychic rules by which the personal feeling of the "I" can be delimited and described. This will be accomplished by this method of pre-arranged introspections that, at its description, might be taken as the only true and sensible constitution of the self.

A second important intention to be found in these pages is to unify findings in psychology, philosophy and the natural sciences into one body of cognitive and perceptive knowledge. Here, an all-important idea is established: that mental mechanisms show their constant function as the laws of physical phenomena show their invariable character. Unfortunately, whereas observation of external physical phenomena yields an impressive amount of scientific rules that apparently define exactly that which is externally observed, the art of introspection has failed to establish a single rule that can convince all philosophers, psychologists or natural scientists at a time.

A third (controversial) general intention to be established is that physicality, the thing-in-itself, can be *perceptively* traced after all. That the idea of an a priori format of the mind can be dogmatically defined, an input and output of fact established, and a trace-back attained that projectionally defines the external world that exists for itself and by itself. The general character of the natural world will be tentatively defined and a process will be suggested that links cognition to true phenomenal happening. It is certain that the mind will never know the real natural world as the world knows itself; perhaps it will know the real natural world as it functions to establish one of its natural priorities—the human being.

Successful scientific results are usually due to the advancement of science's technically developed languages and nomenclatures. These have shown steadiness and apparent universality, and have always been identified by the processes that they intended to describe. As is the case with some features of Quantum Mechanics and Atomic Physics, the unreal character of the language used has been the enlightening value that permits the explanation of an otherwise inexplicable reality. Here, precise mathematical formulations are produced because they agree with artificially developed mathematical "operators", and formulas arise that precede the actual technical findings. The use of algebraic operators is used in a similar way in this treatise to explain *artificially* a psychic reality that the mind cannot see; following this path, we copy the principles of Quantum Mechanics as it develops the mechanics of Atomic Physics. To use the idea of these mathematical operators, together with the basic laws of Matrix Algebra, served the purpose of establishing perception-cognition patterns as understandable constructive processes that clearly detail mind function. The development of these ideas, operators and matrices brings forth two hypotheses that are basic toward a mechanistic approach to understanding: (a) *that consciousness has an existence of its own* and (b) that our mental processes have mechanisms that are fairly constant in their function of observing different phenomena. These ideas, together with a new outlook of the idea of a concept, time and space, produce an interesting and different view of old problems in the field of human understanding.

Propositions are stated without considering specific acts of apprehension of external physical phenomena; the particular experience of the color *red* will not occupy our time, but the general mental process by which we realize the phenomenon of colors will be analyzed. A distinction is assumed between mental state and mental process, the supposition being made that the former has an existence of its own. These propositions are limited to the function of three mental mechanisms—consciousness, imagination and intuition—for they can form the basic constitution of the human mind. The ever-present aim was to find a common denominator to that which makes philosophical truth, psychological findings and scientific rule one and the same under a functional understanding that is hidden but present in all human production.

The main idea in the first chapter is as follows. (a) Whatever it is that forms a single concept has already indicated in itself multiple unimaginable relations to other concepts: (b) what establishes the concept *atom* has to allow for what makes the concept *galaxy*, and such a labyrinthine connection is considered a *fait accompli* by the whole of nature in a timeless way. In general, the human (myopic) stand in front of such a continuous nature gives way to vector-scalar blurrings typical of human cognition.

In the second chapter, an inverse type of mental mechanism is proposed that avoids the general naming of psychic phenomena according to a theory of knowledge; common terms such as Consciousness, Imagination, Memory are first defined functionally and then used as psychic facts. Final philosophical conclusions and not the mathematical means are the ones to be considered in this chapter. Mathematical thought, in the end, must seek the protective shadow of philosophy.

In the third chapter the general idea of inversiveness is developed and the graphical properties of this inversive type of cognition are described.

In the fourth chapter the idea of Uncertainty, as described in physical theory, is generalized into a constant mental mechanism, and given a broader philosophical and psychological basis. Uncertainty could have been developed as a philosophical theory before being used as a physico-mathematical fact. Broad implications could have been developed cognitively, to be finally sustained by the particular physico-mathematical derivations. In these pages, Uncertainty is described as a basic property of the mind. The principles of Cognitive Hyperbolism are also introduced in this chapter and they find their way, finally, into a cosmological theory (Chapter 7).

In the fifth chapter, Memory and Reading are described. They serve as examples for testing the results of the previous Cognitive Theory, and show how the process of *disconnection* allows for the proper function of such a theory.

In the sixth chapter the mathematical mechanism of the Dirac delta function is introduced as uniquely cognitive in character; this cognitive mechanism agrees with the basic ideas of non-Euclidean Geometry. Time and Space are defined in a way that hopefully describe some of the man-nature relationships.

The last chapter is a mathematical analysis of the uncontracted Riemann-Christoffel curvature tensor. The theory in the previous five chapters is used to explain certain mathematical oddities that appear to be present in cognitive observations, such as the advance of the perihelion of Mercury and the deflection of a light beam in the vicinity of the sun's surface. This chapter and the Appendix can be omitted in a first reading.

It is doubtful that one of the objectives of the creation of the human mind was to analyze itself. Certainly, the mechanisms of the mind find their origin in nature, and their final clarification has to be natural. We hope that some light has been found in the proceedings of this treatise to mark the union between man and matter. Here, the only thing that introspection can make out of nature itself is an inspired guess, and perhaps something else phenomenal that could prove to be a boost to our universal destiny.

Chapter 1
Concepts

Knowledge, as consciously enjoyed by man, follows an ever-decreasing existence toward its ultimate creative unity, *the concept*. The cognitive meeting, by the mind, with continuous natural truth is necessary for the formation of the self, where this nature is reduced into a particular psychic form that we label as knowing. The creation of concepts, by the mind, is a cognitive spacing of total homogeneous *phenomena*; it is a process of establishing generalities where only a state of pure universal knowledge exists. Experience of the individual self (unreflecting self) with this continuous stream of homogeneous data brings about conceptual divisions that, through impressions and perceptions, create a seemingly unique Ego. A concept at this stage (when cognitively formed) detaches from itself adhesive factual data that bind it, in a natural-phenomenal way, to other concepts; this adhesive (unconsciously discarded) factual data can be known as the phenomenal substratum. This discarded essence is unavailable to the human cognitive mind.

2 INTRODUCTION TO PROJECTIVE COGNITION

Man is almost totally unaware of the absolute world, for this phenomenal substratum that binds all concepts is without end. Although it is *shown* to us, most of it remains non-cognitive, present in an undelivered sub-conscious world. Will the human mind universally define and totally know all the implications phenomenally contained in the phenomenon called gravity? Is the sensorial phenomenon of pull the only significant phenomenal property of gravity, because it is the only property of the phenomena we can grasp easily?

Our mental structure and its function have been designed in the assumption that the unitarily conceptual observance of our surroundings is safe enough to accomplish an unknown initial creative purpose. The conceptual division mentioned limits the mind to a functional safe existence within the substratum state. This perceptively unconscious area where the clues to natural solutions lie can not be, in most cases, cognitively known. The discovery of some of this prohibited area, and the mathematical relations that will be used to delimit it, will be the subject of this chapter.

Our first step is to re-define the idea of a concept. Classical philosophy usually defines it as a "simple intellectual representation of an object". This definition has certain limitations; adding or substracting qualities will not change its initial simple character. In general this definition (a) is a static cognitive scheme that has to fall into some kind of mental mechanical animation in order to produce a stream of consciousness, (b) has to allow time, in a present state, for recognition in every instance of personal awareness, (c) has to allow time for a succession of units concepts to flow (into a future state) which are somehow traceable back to fractioned lengths of time. But we question, will a successive stream of conceptual flashes produce any kind of meaningful process of cognition? There is no intention at this time to permanently destroy the veracity of this static view of the awareness of a concept, for it helps us in assuming the existence of the mentioned substratum that produces continuity to partial observable facts. But this simple mechanical conceptual progression (as in movies) that the classic philosophical definition of a concept proclaims, is not enough to explain the production of ideas and judgments that are apparently not bound to temporal passage. We have to begin redefining the idea of a concept away from such staticity.

It has been said, "...why is a number, when taken altogether, one?" Why must the number twelve, for example, when taken altogether (as a single concept) have a single meaning? Why does the human mind synthesize in a simple action of awareness the idea of a "dog", retaining it constantly at a cognitive level, when it could have categorized the phenomenon (dog) physiologically down to the last organ or single cell? There is an inherent tendency in the mind to unify qualities, to ignore certain particular relevant facts in order to produce a coherent meaning at a level of safe cognition. This illustrates the basic relation between unending natural data and the human mind in front of it; out of the unstoppable stream of naturality, the mind unvolitionally produces a conceptual flow of cognition that grid-matches that naturality as the safest of all possible approximations. Then, what is ultimately the reality behind awareness? Relegated substratum (each of a million cells) or partial conceptual presence (a dog)? It can be said that the phenomenon of awareness results in a cognitive phenomenal summary that forms the mind's perceptive and behavioral character.

The *assumption* to be proposed now is the following. A conceptual happening, though seemingly beginning and ending in itself, can be divided into two parts, (a) impression, and (b) expression.

The first part, impression, results from the passive meeting of the senses and the passive meeting of the mind with data in a natural state. Husserl expressed the definition of the meaning of Thing as "...a unified and continuous series of possible perceptions which, developed from any one of these, stretch out in an indefinite number of directions in systematic ordered ways, in each direction endlessly, and always dominated throughout by some unity of meaning." The acceptance of this statement could be as follows: that all *possible* perceptions form the continuity of nature, contrary to *actual* perceptions that form the human world. There is disagreement with Husserl's further description of the Thing as mere "...modes of appearing...a nucleus of what is really presented, an outlying zone of apprehension consisting of marginal co-data of an accessory kind, and a more or less vague indeterminacy." This, I believe, belongs to the unconscious substratum previously mentioned that, when apprehended, changes the continuity of natural data into a subconscious state of being. It can be termed accessory (as Husserl did) insofar as it exists in a "parallel" level alongside cognition. A natural datum, the Thing, is continuous, full of all possibilities and totally known beginning from any of its parts. Any of its segments leads finally to any other segment, this being the clue to its definition. The encounter of natural totality, (substratum *and* concept) of perceivable and unperceivable data, between the senses and passive mind constitutes the initial part (impression) of a conceptual happening.

The second part, expression, follows impression. Here, mental mechanisms fragment and condense the final *cognitive* concept and omit the marginal co-data (unconscious perception) previously mentioned. This second part is usually identified with cognition. Cognition, in general, could be explained as following such a dynamic flow in which initial sense impression progresses at a constant pace toward a final stage of human experience.

When we are asked to experience, in an isolated mental happening (we are told to think or imagine only *one* concept), the concept *chair*, it is done as a single mental experience not attached to a true cognitive sequence. The idea of a concept can be readily defined if it is done experimentally and on purpose; when concepts are summoned in a singular form, they manifest themselves clearly, and with their uniqueness. But when the mind experiences a real, everyday cognitive sequence of concepts, devoid of any forced method of insight, then they do not seem to affect us (in a group flow) as they did singly. The concept chair enters into a composed picture of multiple conceptual backgrounds, not bound to fractional time passing and linked, finally, to group and total meaning. This could not be achieved in an add-up cognitive mechanism of successive time-measured concepts. Then, a mental mechanism must be described that can consider a concept to be one thing at a time and another thing at a subsequent cognition. A mental mechanism that will change itself and accept a concept with all its background variants and also accept a concept in its single state; a mechanism with the power of a *pathway* that will allow for impression, transformation and final expression. The purpose of this chapter is to identify such pathways, and some of the laws that characterize them, always identifying their rules with a "spot" recognizing of static conceptual unity.

If it is established that such a pathway follows a simple sense impression—sense expression route, and that a constant mechanism equates, in a yet undefined law, the first *substance-received* apprehension through the senses with a subsequent *substance-given* cognitive expression, then a dynamic way can be built that will give meaning to our first static definition of a concept. The idea of a concept will have a *movable* sense as well as a static sense; a concept will not appear cognitively until it completes a unitary motion through the two-part (impression-expression) pathway.

If this way of reasoning is followed through, the subject of Metaphysics will be forced into an orderly and sensible field of labor. The art of knowing will be oriented from the study of mere opinion into the systemized principles of an established programmatic science. A psychic, scientific-like method can be developed based on a consistent nomenclature that promises multiple single starting points of metaphysical thought to minds that are not necessarily genial, but dogmatic enough to carry on and solve, through persistent work, the unknowns of reflection. "...we have to judge universally on the basis of mere concepts..." says Kant, and he is right, for it is here that the beginning of a new science is found, born out of inspiration and imagination, sometimes casting aside common sense, for common sense at times (as Kant proclaims) "...is capable of no judgment at all." The hidden key to understand cognition is to seek and define phenomena through perception already inside our skull; and this can be done only through intuitive thought that does not intend itself to be taken literally. Only by assuming that a unifying substratum exists at a perceptive-phenomenal level, introducing psychic motional energy into some pathway of the mind, will we be able to answer the above questions.

This pathway identifies something received, something transformed, and something finally produced by an unknown mental mechanism, that will be defined later on. In order to understand the meaning of this second-half pathway, it must be accepted that natural phenomena making impact in our senses are unified and solidly continuous. That their possibilities stretch out in an eternal way, slowly becoming a part of all that exists and that, somehow, the human mind finds a meaning in this continuous stream, which can be apart from any real truth that this continuous stream might finally convey.

If the idea of a concept is considered as a static and easily identified cognition, a confused analysis always determines the inductive result. For example, consider Kant's analytic and synthetic judgments, in which the concepts are superficially labeled. The statement "All bodies are heavy" is a true judgment in the sense that the idea of heaviness relates to the idea of body solely from a standpoint of human determination (we bring together two independently existing concepts), this making them separable; but the statement "All bodies are extended" is no judgment at all, but an *indivisible* identity, natural in origin (a phenomenal fact), that suffers a grammatical dissection into components that do not exist away from each other, just as if we would have considered the statement "All water is water."

When we consider the idea of a concept as if in *motion* and persist in its observation, a conceptual pathway can be easily followed whose description stands out as a basic source of knowing. The cognitive journey of a single concept can be observed, where the grammatical result of seemingly interrelated concepts can be ignored. The laws that rule such a conceptual movement will be presently established.

The following definitions are necessary to illustrate the cognitive pathway that is to be developed.

Definitions

Apprehension. It is defined as the *sensorial* awareness of phenomenal fact. It is the initial external encounter between the senses and physical phenomena.

Perception. It is defined as the end result of the first half of the previously mentioned pathway (substance-received pathway). It is the *product* of this half-pathway where gross apprehension is processed (of possible and impossible cognition, as we shall see).

Cognition. It is defined as the end result of the second half of the mentioned pathway (substance-given pathway). It is symbolic in nature, originating from unconscious perceptive products. It forms the act of immediate knowing.

Phenomena. This term can be identified with the initial physical presentation of data in its plural continuity. A natural object at this stage is the presence of all of its qualities and attributes seen and *unseen* by the senses. Only a fraction of these qualities finds its way into consciousness.

Phenomenon. This term can be identified with the final mental *picture* (with a singular meaning) produced in the final half of the substance-given pathway. It is what *we* make of things; it is the conscious meaning of that small percentage of qualities that makes its way to this final half-pathway.

In this way we part from the mainline of thought seen in previous philosophers who have themselves gone into motion to describe a stationary idea of a concept. We have initiated into motion the very essence of a concept. And we are going to give it a pathway in time, in space, in order to attain a clear description of the forces that produce such a pathway; and from here on we cannot profess any allegiance to previous philosophical establishments. We shall begin the description of this mental cognitive journey by describing the two phases all concepts must follow: *vectoriality* and *scalarity*.

Knowledge begins when we depart from the realities of the natural world, and ends when we re-encounter, on our terms, the same natural phenomena. Man was not created to live by the total and plain facts that phenomena ultimately represent, but was given the ability to expand on them individually, in such a way not to interfere with them (as far as the act of awareness goes) and in no way to change them. Nature is completely oblivious to the presence of man, for the observance of man by nature is nonexistent. The existence of man is not needed for whatever means and ends nature's destiny is pointing at. But to the contrary, the mind of man is dependent on natural ways to be called a mind and exists on the basis of a path that cannot be reversed. Then, what is given to us must be distinguished from what is given by us; any world phenomena given to us cannot be un-world cognitively and, consequently, we must build a scheme that serves the cognitive principles of philosophy, psychology and the natural sciences, not out of *true* phenomena but out of true phenomenon. For what is the reflective mind but that which makes itself one with a parallel responsible nature? For the self is singular, its true nature being that thing that admits but excludes any other self, even nature's self. Only by admitting that mental mechanisms are a path leading out toward singularity of all possible natural plurality, will we attain a clear view of what the self ultimately means. Knowing is a facing away (momentarily) from the fact of nature in order to reencounter it again in a new and personal way; the personal way of color, form, dimension, etc. A coming in and a going out (the cognitive pathway) of the self produced must be defined to understand this nature-man relationship.

Vector and Scalar Concepts

These two terms will be taken from the field of Physics, because they describe accurately the character of the cognitive pathway that is to be developed. Remembering that a vector is defined (in Physics) as having quantity *and* direction, and a scalar is defined as having only quantity, we will use this difference to explain this pathway. The dynamic state to which a concept belongs at the initial half-pathway will be given the name of vectoriality, and the concept at this stage will be known as a *vector concept*. Unapprehended physical phenomena will be known as *natural vectoriality*. All vector concepts are united and point to each other in the sense that any continuum depends on its particular components for its total meaning; from any of its parts all parts will be reached eventually. A vector concept is in a state that can intrinsically imply or indicate those other concepts that are part of the unified and continuous initial physical phenomena apprehended.

Vector concepts (or half-concepts belonging to the first, substance-received pathway) are not conscious. This initial half-pathway contains data that proceed to the second half-pathway and data (substratum) that remain in the stage of perception as we have defined it, both part of a unified unending continuum. The consideration of distances clearly exemplifies this; for the distance between an observer and the moon is there in the presence of the viewer, yet he is unable to assess its exact cognitive value. This information is apprehended but stays vectorially in an uncognitive perception. Vectors have a *genotype* framework that will induce in the mind a hidden (perceptively unconscious) definition of phenomena that might differ from the one we insert (consciously) into nature. In this sense we can state that vectorial concepts may be factually representative of true natural phenomena.

The dynamic state to which a concept belongs at the final half-pathway will be given the name of scalarity, and the concept at this stage will be known as a *scalar concept*. It has a stationary character, devoid of direction or indication and is produced with a self-contained intention. A scalar concept is the result of the substance-given pathway, one that apparently does not imply or indicate other concepts, as it confers a sense of uniqueness, its final and total meaning being itself (the color *red is* absolutely *red*, its *finality* being *red*). It has a phenotype-like framework resulting in substance-given cognition. Scalar concepts are symbolic and *produce all types of consciousness*.

The cognitive balance between vectoriality and scalarity can be viewed as follows: The letter k by itself forms a concept with an identifiable meaning; the name "New York" is by itself a concept and the letter k has been relegated into vectoriality (partial unconsciousness) existent in the first part of the pathway. The statement "It rains in New York" can be taken by itself as a concept (as a single representation of a happening), and the letter k has then been relegated into further vectoriality (it almost disappears). The whole cognitive pathway responds instantly, producing *single* scalar concepts whose components might be concepts by themselves but are relegated in this particular instance to some form of vectoriality. The previous example can be projected to visual experience, auditory experience, and tactile experience.

The Cognitive Inversion

In what way is the conceptual journey through this pathway (phenomena present, substance-received, substance-given, final cognition) accomplished? This is an unknown process whose true mechanism will always be hidden to us. As an alternative toward total knowledge, the human mind can not look upon itself, for it lacks the power for that perspective; a recognizing gap cannot be built into the process. We can only guess, time and time again (philosophy after philosophy), until the last scheme more akin to human understanding appears. The assumptions that will follow in this treatise are based on the observation that phenomena, solidly continuous, are transformed into particular meaning by the mind; the schemes that explain this are, to my belief, the simplest forms that could be found in order to convey, objectively and to the point, what cognitive inversion means. And these schemes are based on the following. From natural quantitative *chaos*, the mind produces a cognitive inversion that results in a qualitative orderly view that is in touch with the initial quantitative nature. We are going to guess that this vector-scalar cognitive route, this phenomena-phenomenon process possesses the character of an *inversion*. Somehow the inversion pathway resembles the left-to-right transposition seen in a mirror. In this kind of inversion there is no quantitative change, but there is a qualitative transformation, this being similar to vector-scalar concept formation.

Let us ask ourselves, what significance can a part of nature attain in front of another part of nature? What could a perceptible object, in front of a piece of its own kind, rigidly aware beforehand of all possibilities—what could such a thing make out of a happening of which everything is known from every particular stance? Husserl's internal and external horizons in the phenomenon of cognition would cease to exist in this complex relation because what is effectually perceived from a particular situation always appears in the light of data that is also perceived from every other particular situation. Nature in front of nature is characterized by the absence of any phenomenological *noema* (as defined by Husserl). Then we have the human mind, faced with the same particular situation, in front of the same quantitative data presented to the initial segment of nature; when we perceive the phenomenon of a "car", the visual apprehension is only one aspect of it (be it front, the back or the side), though the general cognition has a complete significance. This is so because basic concepts have an *instantaneous* threshold of recognition, whereupon a segment of the final concept will give cognition of the whole meaningful concept (the entire car, not the front, back or side only). The human mind has developed the character of meaning in response to its inability of attaining total knowledge in front of nature, since nature in front of nature would need no meanings. A quantitative background (substratum) is accepted immediately (not necessarily at the level of consciousness) of all data presented and acknowledged in the *substance-received* half-pathway. Then it is passed on as unconscious quantitative background into the *substance-given* half-pathway. This background or substratum is always apart, marginal (and yet parallel), from the meaning that allows us cognition. The space that the "car" occupies is part of that ignored substratum. The true quantitative nature of every concept remains throughout the whole pathway, with a *qualitative* transformation obtained parallel to this *quantitative* background. We seem to scalarize only the available initial view. In this way imaginary artificial recalls *out of any context* can be brought to life because of this quantitative background that is preserved and allowed to reform the cognitive substance of imagination.

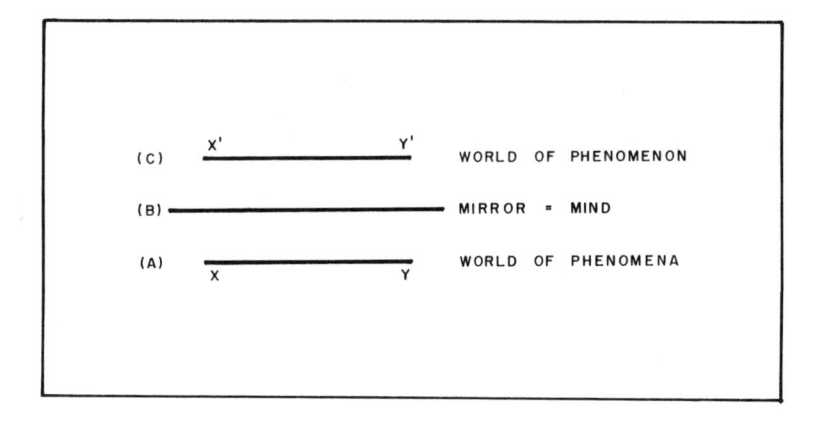

```
(C)   X'―――――Y'         WORLD OF PHENOMENON

(B)   ―――――――――         MIRROR = MIND

(A)   ―――――――――         WORLD OF PHENOMENA
       X        Y
```

Figure 1. Phenomena (XY) transpose directionally into Y^1X^1, producing a *cognitive* qualitative difference, but the absolute value XY is still equal to X^1Y^1.

Let us examine what happens in a mirror-like cognitive image; such an inversive scheme can be illustrated graphically if the observer is always human, as in Figure 1, page 11. Here we see that (a) $X = Y^1$ and $Y = X^1$ in an inverse way and (b) the essential meaning of X is in Y^1 and of Y is in X^1. (c) X progresses into a cognitive Y^1 and Y progresses into a cognitive X^1. The following is also observed: $XY = X^1Y^1$ quantitatively and $XY = Y^1X^1$ qualitatively.

Cognition can be considered an A to C inverse route and vectoriality an A to B half-route that does not yield cognition by itself. Scalarity is a B to C route that yields cognition, while vectoriality is a *factual* half-route of incoming phenomena (this determined by the inadequacy of our senses).

In Figure 1, page 11, XY is all that our sensorium can *observe* out of phenomena. This is shown to our mind, which *sees* Y^1X^1 symbolically out of XY and ultimately out of the whole incoming natural phenomena. A simpler, graphical representation of the inversion can be seen in Figure 2, page 13.

Either way, true natural reality keeps away from us in two ways: (a) because of limited sensorial acuteness that prevents observation of continuous phenomena. Here what seeps through is still vectoriality. (b) By the inversive act that transforms this later vectoriality into symbolic scalar meaning. Natural vectoriality is the source of all scalarity. Nature has a total view (macrocosmically and microcosmically) of the whole phenomenal world; the necessity of an inversion would be a handicap, an obstruction that, to the human mind, guarantees *the* functional being amid the infinity of phenomenal detail. Then, a phenomenal act is devoid of cognition, and cognition cannot define that act.

Vectorial Concepts

Definition. A vectorial concept can be defined as an apprehension that can be oriented in an unlimited way toward other apprehensions. It is multidirectional. Two kinds of vector concepts can be defined in the first half of the cognitive pathway: (a) the one where incomplete apprehension of phenomena is attained because of poor sensorial qualities. It is still vectorial datum born out of vectorial data not yet

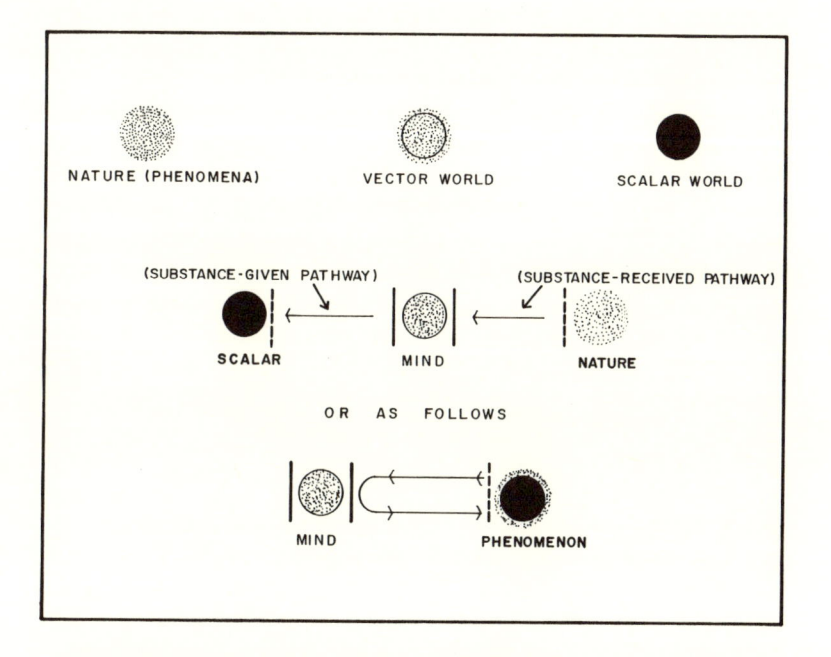

Figure 2. Phenomena undergo a U-track *back* into their own being, as phenomenon. A substance-received pathway *returns conceptually through a substance-given pathway.*

14 INTRODUCTION TO PROJECTIVE COGNITION

scalarized, part of its totality bound to be relegated. (b) The one where phenomena are not fragmented sensorially, because they have the character of being all or none apprehensively. Here again, part of the phenomena will be conceptually relegated at final scalar formation. These are basic natural processes like gravity, mass, etc. These concepts become conscious when forced to appear (as in the previous example of the concept *chair*) but in actual, real cognition they remain unconscious.

Coalitionative property of vector concepts. Vectorial concepts can be traced into a continuum of *happening*, their relations to one another found to be perfectly coalitionative. True natural meaning can be found only by being able to observe all implications that come from or result from a single vectorial concept, this in all possible directions. If we have a vector concept :a:, where : : indicates vectoriality, and a vector concept :b:, both concepts part of a phenomenal reality :a:b:, and our senses will only register :a: as a cognitive reality, the following relation results:

Equation #1

:a:b: ↔ :a:

where the broken line : between a and b is indicative coalition. This is the first important Phenomenal Proposition stated, its relevance further discussed in Chapter 6. The phenomenal reality :a:b: indicates :a: and :a: indicates :a:b: at all times, where indication (↔) means an immediate, unique compromise between two concepts that *cannot be substituted*. Equation #1 occurs in the first part of the pathway (substance-received) and it proceeds on an unconscious level, as stated. In a coalition :a:b:, both :a: and :b: will hold their character in either form (as :a:, :b:, or :a:b:) as if they were the same. Vectorially, :a: (or :b:) *is* :a:b:, and :a:b: will be in :a: (or :b:). Coalition is explicitly present in :a:b: and implicitly present in :a: (or :b:) alone. When :a: is pushed forward into substance-given, it *apparently* loses its coalition to :b:, together with the cognition (not the apprehension) of :b:, since :b: remains uncognitive in the substance-received pathway in coalition as :a:b:. An example of this would be the cognition of any object and the space it occupies, e.g., airplane = :a:, and the positional space it occupies is equal to :b:.

Scalar Concepts

Definition. A scalar concept is defined as any cognitive phenomenon that will only indicate itself. It has no direction. Two kinds of scalar concepts can be defined: (a) the one that results from the fragmented apprehension of (vectorial) phenomena. Its contents are basic vectoriality plus human-made meaning. They can be regarded as a *conversion* resulting from the apprehension of vectoriality. (b) The one that could result from the *conversion* of all-or-none apprehended phenomena, possible only in *pure* basic natural processes.

Aggregative property of scalar concepts. Scalar concepts are aggregative. If we have a scalar concept /a/, where / / stands for scalarity and a scalar concept /b/, both part of a phenomenon reality /a/b/, the following relation results:

Equation #2

$$/a/ + /b/ \rightleftarrows /a/b/$$

where / between a and b is indicative of aggregation. Conscious logical products are *additive* in a scalar way and all scalar cognition exists self contained.

By definition,

/a/b/ → /a/ and
/a/b/ → /b/

but

Equation #3

/a/ |→| /a/b/
/b/ |→| /a/b/

16 INTRODUCTION TO PROJECTIVE COGNITION

since /a/ or /b/ will never be indicative of /a/b/. Example: The concept *car* can point to a color (*red*), but the concept *red* does not necessarily point to the concept *car*. The / / symbol in Equation #3, page 15, represents *no* indication.

Equation #4

/a/ ↔ 0
/b/ ↔ 0

define a scalar concept as one of self-indicative isolation. They are additive in an algebraic unitary way.

It is not possible to coalesce a vectorial concept and a scalar concept and it is impossible to aggregate a vectorial concept and a scalar concept. In Equation #2, page 15, neither /a/ or /b/ alone will be indicative of /a/b/, for the relation between them is only aggregative. All possible human cognition is aggregative (scalar) and the world of exterior phenomena is in total coalition.

Examples of vector and scalar concepts. If the sum $4 + 5 = 9$ is considered as an example of a presumed vectorial happening (which in reality cannot be, because then that possibility could not be cognitively possible) for illustrative purposes, then a phenomenal whole (without parts) can be changed to a scalar-like scheme whose sum is the sum of its parts. Two different observers have to be considered in front of the same vectoriality; one that sees phenomena as they exactly exist, and another one that perceives phenomena where data omission results in cognition.

In this artificial scalar make-up of false vectoriality, type (a) vectors are considered which, in our daily living, are the most numerous. Type (b) vector concepts are not prone to artificial vector setups for they cannot suffer fragmentation in their homogeneous (repetitive) all-or-none character. Here, an artifical scheme would have to be coalitionative-like and not additive, since their homogeneity would show the same face to the two observers. The sum $4 + 5 = 9$ is the simplest example that can be reduced to an artificial vector scheme; any kind of common judgment could be be reduced to this vectorial make-up situation.

Analytic judgments, in the manner of Kant's analysis, represent a repetitive type (:a:a:) of coalition where the indicative property of vectoriality has been cognitively (grammatically) resolved. They can only attain *one* specific degree of scalar formation. They are not amenable to artificial vectorial make-ups, hence they come from type (b) vectorial concepts. Synthetic (Kantian) judgments are easily reduced to this type of make-up vectoriality, for between their concepts (:a:b:) abound indicative factors that are *easily* observed when a second observer is placed in the vectorial perspective. They tend to rise from type (a) vectorial concepts.

If the + 5 = 9 part of the sum is hidden to our first observer (scalar observer) then,

Example 1(a)

$$4 \left[+ \quad 5 \quad = \quad 9 \right] \leftarrow \text{hidden}$$

This specific number 4, which is the only thing apparent to the scalar observer (the other numbers hidden), cannot stand by itself as a generality and will always be indicative of the sum 9 as long as the point of view of observer number two (vectorial observer) exists. The sum has been omitted knowingly and voluntarily, this sum remaining as a hidden proof of the commitment of that particular 4. It is part of a vectorial setup and can not be used apart from itself as a general concept (this because of the vectorial point of view). It only seems so because the scalar observer categorizes it in the printed form of *his* general concept of the number 4. When the second observer cannot be set apart from the first, judgments, like the one above, tend to be synthetic. Consciousness realigns itself with the scalar point of view. As the idea of general meaning grows cognitively (one dozen, one million, a week, a year, etc.) the possibility of a vectorial observation practically disappears.

If the sum 4 + 0 = 4 is considered, then

Example 1(b)

$$4 \left[+ \quad 0 \quad = \quad 4 \right] \leftarrow \text{hidden}$$

This number 4 will be only indicative of itself, *the* number 4, for it does not participate in additional information to the vectorial observer; actually, it would appear *different* to that vectorial observer. The hidden proof created will not be indicative of something different. Furthermore, if any kind of judgment is considered to be the mental mechanical expression of a single concept relation, then the above reasoning applies to recognized single concepts and to recognized single judgments, for they are no more than singular concepts grammatically dissected.

The number 4, in Example 1(a), participated in a setup that binds it vectorially in a permanent way and would disappear except for the fact that it is repetitive. No generality of its being exists phenomenally. The number 4 in Example 1(b) did not participate in any compromise, only in itself, and this makes it a symbolic scalar concept. As in example 1(a), 4s are individually committed in all external phenomena. They are engaged specifically in this or that action, part of a phenomenal continuum, involved always in a phenomenal truth. When they are repetitive, they define the essence of the continuity of nature. Vectorial repetition defines universal simultaneity and the character of that eternity present in our minds. The whole significance of nature can be traced from any of them. The general concept of *a* number 4 does not exist phenomenally (or in phenomena, in nature). Human cognition, on the contrary, is finite. Here we aggregate final and seemingly conclusive concepts that correspond *inversely* to vectorial concepts, and we clump them into general definitions as if they did not belong to a specific happening.

Scalar concept formation involves the unitary fragmentation that results from an undefined inversion that changes perception into a unique and edited phenomenon. And a phenomenon with energy that tends toward the formation of *whole* scalar ideas that advance from single scalarity to multiple scalarity. This is human thought and ideas. Scalarity, in general, turns abstractly into a form of general cognition that progressively ignores the unit scalar that formed it, building up pieces of real phenomenon and thought. This is in contrast to vectoriality that turns progressively into a micro-world, losing meaning after meaning toward total anonymity. To go after what remains hidden of an observed fact would be to involve ourselves in a *dissolution* of our functional ability to create meanings.

Concepts 19

What we do, as observers, is to stop momentarily a continuous flow of unending specificity and cognitively begin another flow of personal generalities that allows individual existence. The scalar world is a protective screen in front of totality; it is staticity in the form of fragmentary unity, and to scalarize in a direction is to give meaning (inverse) to flow of happening that changes its character when it suffers such a transformation.

Simple Inverse Algebra

Symbolic definitions. The following are symbolic expressions that explain an inversive act:

(a) 0^- defines an observer.

(b) Cv_0 defines total phenomenal reality.

(c) Cv defines phenomena through the senses. They are vectorial concepts.

(d) Cv_1 defines *non-cognitive* phenomenal reality present in the first half of the cognitive pathway. It is the substratum that the mind selects in unconsciousness, like the space the car occupied in the previous example. It is a fraction of the total Cv.

(e) Cv_2 defines *pre-cognitive* phenomenal reality present in the first half of the cognitive pathway. This will proceed to the second half-pathway to produce cognition. It forms the remaining fraction of the total Cv.

(f) OCv defines the initial encounter of phenomena with a particular observer.

(g) OCv_1 defines *non-cognitive* reality in the first half of the cognitive pathway, already a part of a particular observer (though unconsciously relegated). Non-Euclidean meanings belong here.

(h) OCv_2 defines *pre-cognitive* reality in the first half of the cognitive pathway, already a part of a particular observer (this part will be consciously relevant).

(i) Cs defines a scalar phenomenon coming exclusively from Cv_2. It has a general meaning common to *all* observers.

(j) OCs defines cognition of a particular observer, coming exclusively from OCv_2. It is the final product that dictates behavior.

20 INTRODUCTION TO PROJECTIVE COGNITION

Algebraic cognitive possibilities.

1. *First possibility.*

Equation #5

$0^{--} + Cv_0 = OCv$

where Cv_0 becomes Cv.

This shows the simple presentation of total phenomenal reality to an observer resulting in fractional sensorial apprehension. Here the following is proposed:

Equation #6

$Cv = :Cv_1:Cv_2:$
$Cv \neq Cv_1 + Cv_2$

which states the fact that what is apprehended *per se* forms a coalitionative relation, not an additive one. Then we have

Equation #7

$OCv = (OCv_1)(OCv_2)$

which states that the observer's mental mechanisms transform factual apprehended coalition into an *inverse* mathematical relation. *This is the first hypothetical property of* 0^{--}. Equation #7 allows the following:

(a) the possibility of an infinitely large degree of precognition versus an infinitely small degree of vectoriality, and vice versa (this is assuming that OCv is constant for all observers);

(b) the presence of vectorial universal simultaneity (its unending continuum) in the presence of an almost absent pre-cognitive 0^{--};

(c) expanded *feeling* by 0^{--} (as in *straight* phenomena, e.g., gravity, mass, space, etc.) toward vectorial simultaneity, in the presence of a small Cv_1;

(d) established cognition amid a multiplicative relation.

Since OC_{V_2} proceeds totally to OCs, we can substitute it in Equation #7 and we have:

Equation #8

$OCv = (OCv_1)(OCs)$

This expresses the philosophical fact that cognitive and non-cognitive apprehension vary inversely with each other. Total apprehended phenomena (OCv) are assumed to be constant.

Our behavior is determined by OCs. It expands at the expense of OCv_1 but not at the expense of OCv. If OCv is taken as a phenomenal unitary constant (assuming that sensorial report is constant) then,

Equation #9

$(OCv_1)(OCs) = k$

where k is equal to a unitary constant and to OCv.

2. *Second possibility.*

Equation #10

$OCv = OCs$
$OCv = OCv_1$

if OCv_1 and OCs reach a unitary limit respectively. That is, OCv_1 = vectorial unity in the first relation in Equation #10 and OCs = scalar unity in the second relation in Equation #10.

If it is assumed that Equation #10 alternates both of its members in some kind of repetitive process (through *disconnection*, as will be shown later), then the alternate viewing seen in the famous Boring Figure can be explained (see Figure #3, page 23). Here if the old woman is scalar, the young woman remains uncognitively vectorial and vice versa. From the vectorial point of view none exist; from the

22 INTRODUCTION TO PROJECTIVE COGNITION

scalar point of view both exist in a *time* sequence. If we use Equation #10, page 21, to explain the Boring Figure, the result would be as follows (OCs_1 is equal to the particular cognition of the young lady, OCs_2 is equal to the particular cognition of the old lady, OCv_1 is equal to a non-cognition of a particular observer, Cs_1 is equal to the *general* concept of the young lady, Cs_2 is equal to the *general* concept of the old lady):

(a) $OCv = OCs_1$ where OCv_1 is equal to vectorial unity and Cs_2 is a part of Cv_1 (there is cognition of the young lady), or,

(b) $OCv = OCv_1$ where OCs_1 and OCs_2 are unity (no cognition), or,

(c) $OCv = OCs_2$ where OCv_1 is equal to vectorial unity and Cs_1 is a part of Cv_1 (there is cognition of the old lady).

This leads to the following cognitive *balance*,

$$OCs_1 \leftrightarrow OCv_1 \leftrightarrow OCs_2$$

but since OCv_1 is non-cognitive, the process reduces itself to

$$OCs_1 \leftrightarrow OCs_2$$

which is the common cognitive experience. In some observers OCv_1 might predominate where neither the young or the old lady would be recognized (as in *b* above) and a non-Euclidean factor might appear.

Cause and Effect

This is another example where we can apply the results of the cognitive inversion. The observance of the phenomenon of cause and effect can be explained if we have an event of the type of Equation #1, page 14, followed by an event of the type of Equation #10, page 21. Assuming that a vectorial continuum :a:b: is identified in a scalar way through a $T_1 T_2$ directional time span (directional and positional time will be explained in Chapter 2), then,

:a:b: $\rightarrow a$ *cognitively* in T_1

where *a* is identifed with a cause, and,

:a:b: → b   *cognitively* in T$_2$
where *b* is identified with an effect.

Figure 3. Ambiguous figure from E. Boring. Published in 1930.

This progressive change follows Equation #10, page 21, in its alternate direction. What we see in the Boring Figure (Figure #3, above) is the same phenomenon that we find in the cognition of cause and effect with the difference that in Figure #3 we cannot identify anything common between the two ladies. This particular young lady, and none other will always follow the cognition of the old lady, and none other. And that is exactly what happens in the phenomenon of cause and effect.

Chapter 2
Thematic Field Theory

Categories, as envisioned by Kant, are structures that come from *a priori* thought; they are a priori concepts completely independent of and prior to experience. Experience is secondary, and is needed only for the auto-encounter of the self as a source of order and differentiation in front of the general function of consciousness. But, one may ask, in what form do these categories exist, between what limits can they perform, and what percentage of apriori thought do they represent? Are they part of a psychic mechanism or do they spontaneously appear when needed, as general concepts do?

Husserl goes one step further, describing the subjective duality of possession (experienced as *mine*, thus a two object relation) as related to the appearence of "me" as a *fundamental fact* (Urtatsache). He recognizes a *transcendental* field of pure experience available only through reflective analysis, denying the possibility of the existence of the self for and by itself. The "I" as a fundamental substance will only exist (or be produced) in front of undefinable phenomena, a world (the "I") intended only in front of another world that actually does not *pre-exist*, but that is necessary for its scalar existence. But how can the self exist as always the same in the presence of different phenomena? How can multiple kinds of self arise, in front of the same phenomena? How can a cognitive mechanism exist if this mechanism *appears* only as a continuous test of itself?

In order to answer the above questions, a few basic assumptions and propositions will be discussed in the following paragraphs. They are intended to clarify and delimit the cognitive problems discussed in this chapter. They are stated in six general cognitive intentions.

First: Let us assume the existence of a simple mechanism of cognition related to the process of perception and apprehension, and let us try to avoid identifying isolated, partial, mental processes as whole general structures of mind function. Let us identify such things as Imagination, Consciousness, Memory in a *functional* way so that we do not establish them as self-evident phenomenon, trying to avoid their use as well-defined facts in introspective search.

Second: The a priori labeling of particular mental production has to be identified with a constant mental mechanism where categories are a common denominator. The transcendental union of experience and self will be accepted as sufficient for the personal existence of the "I", but will not be necessary for the existence of the self *at all times*.

Third: What will be proposed follows in the steps of Husserl's *eidetic reduction* and not his phenomenological reduction. A path will be defined that goes from particular (individual) conception of phenomena to conceptions of phenomenon that include the production of empirical generalities. If these reach (though they do not have to) a stage of ultimate phenomenal presupposition, it will have to be considered an advanced step of the eidetic reduction and then called phenomenological reduction.

Fourth: *It will be denied that consciousness is intentional at all times*. The idea that consciousness has to be the awareness of something at all times is not acceptable. Here a distinction must be made between a conscious act, which almost always confronts us with *objects* (as correctly defined by Brentano, and subsequently expanded by Husserl to ideal, real, existent or imaginary objects), and the *general act* of consciousness. There exists a potential "consciousness of..." psychic scheme, at all times present, that contains, but is apart from, conscious acts per se. If the nature of this "consciousness of..." can be defined successfully, then we can dispose of any preformed "sensible qualities" of the mind that coincide with the actual experience perceived. If a background can be built, not of specific qualities but of the time and space that they exclusively and repeatedly occupy in their mental existence (as will be defined in the chapter that deals with memory), then a functional analysis can be developed of the mechanisms of consciousness, instead of explaining each conscious act as a unique and separate happening. This could be taken as the permanent continuous *noematic* character in every perception as conceived by Husserl, where a corresponding act of consciousness disappears but the time-space background remains. A continuous stream of perception can be produced going through this type of time-space *noema*.

Heidegger's pre-cognitive awareness where a preconceptual understanding of being exists seems equal to the above idea but differs from our conception of consciousness as follows. (a) The act of consciousness (*noesis*) is not always directed toward the intentional object (*noema*), precisely this being the outstanding feature of a potential "consciousness of..." mechanism, and (b) this preconceptual awareness is mechanistic in nature, away from the *Mood* (Stimmung) that Heidegger identifies with modifications of melancholy, fear, anxiety, despair, etc.

Fifth: The perceiving quality of the act that will be described will dispense with intentionality and still adapt consciousness, when it happens, to phenomena outside itself in a time sequence of the mentioned potentiality and the act of consciousness per se. The phenomenal world that induces and lies beyond consciousness, when visualized and described by mental mechanisms, continues its existence as a continuous substratum of unconscious function that behaves *as if* consciousness were a conceptual spacing of its continuous meaning. But since we cannot (as humans) consider, or be aware of, the fact that consciousness is a phenomenon of omission (substratum relegated), we cannot proclaim, through the normal sense of cognition, the existence of this substratum full of gaps that denies intentionality.

The following theory is descriptive and follows what is psychologically observed. It will try to explain physical, philosophical and psychological rules and unite these three subjects under one theory of knowledge. As all philosophical theories, it is a personal production;

it assumes that the real truth of mental function is apprehensively prohibited to that same mental function. It is an attempt to explain from *within*, thus an introspective philosophy.

Sixth: The general act of cognition follows a pattern of function that is unaffected from one type of cognition to another. The process of *viewing* cognitively a tree at a distance, an airplane in motion, a familiar face can be related to *a certain constant phenomenon* of awareness. To recognize a familiar landscape under the same terms over and over again points to some underlying permanent mechanism that will not change its function throughout the repeated phenomena. There is a mechanism whose essential nature is to unfold some sort of constant screen that accepts phenomena, framing it out into the privileged condition of cognition. The possibility of description of particular phenomena stops here, and a constant *selective* screen of awareness takes over behind the cognitive purpose of every mind-phenomena encounter. It is as if a potentiality of apprehension existed *prior* to the encounter act, dissolved into the act at the time of cognition.

The function of this pre-present screen, as we shall call it, is to adjust incoming patterns of phenomena in a regular and predictable sense. This cognitive screen serves in the manner of a *mathematical operator*, always acting as a mediating tool, but not as the final conceptual fact produced. It may be present (or expectant) when the actual process of cognition is absent, and operate when the challenge of phenomena is present. It remains in a dormant state, contrary to the non-functional act of sleep, in potentiality to produce cognition when challenged. This is the central idea on which a Thematic Field Theory will be developed.

Mental Operators

Mental operators are basic self-existing mechanisms, identified normally with the actual "I" human condition, and unaffected by interaction wth phenomena. They persist in potentiality even in the absence of undefinable phenomena. Their characteristics are fundamental and form the psychology of mental dynamics. This assumption of the existence of consciousness in the absence of any incoming data gives way to the possibility of a study of psychology on the basis of a *disconnected* function of the mind.

The character of these operators is unique; their presence must remain hidden from the same self that they produce, they must engage in activities where their mediation is only inferred and not positively asserted. They will form the essence of Husserl *eidetic reduction* that takes away the "I" from the simple datum in a motion toward general data. They create in the meantime the seemingly *empty* (unfelt) character of the self. Their objective identity progresses into a subjective representation of *conceptual notion*, this side by side with the unchanged existence of continuous vectorial phenomena. Their groundwork will be assumed to be that of a *space-time screen* creating a uniformity of function that will allow constancy in proposing general cognitive laws.

If, following Kant's example, we picture an object in space, and piece by piece we imaginatively remove it, we cannot remove mentally the residual space (or time) of such an object-happening. But, if we imagine an object in space and time, *we cannot separate from it its empty vicinity*. The residual space-time complex (of Kant's example) and the empty vicinity are constantly present in the form of a screen that identifies the mental operators, in this case, the "consciousness of..." operator. From now on such a screen will be referred to as a *thematic field*.

The form of a thematic field is always linked to a particular approach of the mind (time lapse is recognized mainly as an auditory route, space a visual or tactile route) though they are always uniform in a space-time sense. The most frequently used type of a thematic field is the visual-pictorial kind that we have identified as "consciousness of..." Another thematic field is that of the imagination responding as if its time-space screen were willfuly variable. And still another type of a thematic field that will be briefly discussed in this work is that of the intuition that responds to a *positional* (absolute) type of time and space. All thematic fields consist of inter-related time and space in one of two ways: (a) Expectantly (expectant visually when we are imagining or expectant intuitively when we are reasoning) in a potential way. Present, but not active. (b) Cognitively when in an actual conceptual process. They differ in their specific space-time configuration, and when *mixed* thematic fields occur (as will be shown) it is in an active cognitive process, not in an expectant state.

The next mathematical assumption to be made in order to explain the human mind will be the following; all the laws of Matrix Algebra apply to mental operators, and all thematic fields can be expressed as a time-space matrix as follows,

$$\begin{pmatrix} - & X \\ Y & - \end{pmatrix}$$

where X = space and Y = time. Time and space are inter-related into the matrix in the manner of individual components that uniformly fill this *screen-matrix* in a constant manner and not as individual concepts that define specific phenomena. A single cognitive route through its function reduces itself unitarily to the concept; and the inception of such a concept ends in its all-or-none character. Innumerable vector-relegated concepts might accompany a single cognitive route, but one concept will result that encompasses (vectorially) all of them.

This approach is only an artificial mathematical framework that, in the assumption that such mind work or constitution cannot be empirically delucidated (as is the case with Atomic Physics and its unreal language, Quantum Mechanics), will help explain basic mental function without actual deductive tests as those found in psychological experimental methods. Throughout the development of the present method, philosophical explanations are intended, relations and formulas being only tools that help explain these phenomena much better. The aim is to develop a philosophy out of established science, and finally to state that scientific thought is nothing else but a singular character of mind function that *creates* scientific laws. What is intended is nothing else but to explain general mental patterns and not specific individual happenings of cognition.

Of all the laws of matrix algebra that are valid, the laws of sum and multiplication are the most useful. In general, perception-cognition patterns can be either intentional (volitive) or non-intentional (non-volitive). Intentional perception-cognition patterns occur *at will*, being mainly deductive or reasoned acts that follow non-intentional perception-cognition patterns. They show step (additive) matriceal progression. Non-intentional perception-cognition patterns are not volitive, always passive (contemplative) and self-effacing; they show a multiplicative matriceal progression. We will be dealing mainly with this last type of perception-cognition patterns.

Thematic field operators. Thematic field operators, as described, have the following properties: (a) Their function is *partial* at the meeting with phenomena due to the scalar cognitive inversion described previously and to the shortcomings of the sensorial apparatus. When recognizing the general concept of "dog" the mind partially removes from it what in another cognition the concept of "eye" would be the principal issue. This concept of an "eye" is particularly relegated to *non-cognition* in the general concept of "dog." Another example is the following: when we sensorially fail to appreciate correct distances (as from an observer to the moon) or fractional measures of time (as in fractions of a second). In this last instance the correct quantitative appreciation is there to see but the observer grossly misjudges it. In both these examples the operator permits expectancy of further vectoriality involved, but it is not relevant to the production of the actual human concept that results; it is actually a no-reporting of data that can be recorded under a different perception-cognitive pattern. The response of these operators seems to go from a general type of cognition at first to greater specific cognition at a subsequent time; it is safer for the species to appreciate first in a total way and then go to particulars. (b) Apprehension, as normally recorded, impresses a *boundary-like* tract where *blind spots* exist (to be defined later on) leaving a horizon-like mark of *hypersensitivity* (equal to the "icon" memory described in psychological experiments). Here, further possibilities of positional time and space exist, allowing for micro and macro states present in uncognitive vectoriality and guessed in imaginative and intuitive thinking. It can be described as the site that exists between *unremoveable* space (Kant's example) and its space vicinity. Since "we" are the actual operator, its function will always remain hidden as a background, present *with or without* phenomenal confrontation; the boundary-like phenomenon delimits and heralds the thematic field existence (*our* existence).

(c) All cognition through operators, after initial apprehension, remains for a time *as if* phenomena were still reporting themselves, creating a duration for the hypersensitivity described. (d) When the thematic field is expectant (as in *a* above) and not in active recording, it is always two-dimensional. Three dimensions appear only when the operator is affected; if we remove imaginatively a three-dimensional phenomenon part by part, what remains is a two-dimensional *matrix screen*.

Time and space. This topic will be discussed in Chapter 6. What follows is an introductory summary necessary for the discussion of mental operators. There are three different types (or modalities) to what we call cognitive time and space that are of concern in the interaction of matrix operators. They are *objective*, *variable* and *positional* time and space.

1. Objective time and space. These are the ones we refer to in every day living and the ones we ascribe to all natural phenomena. Our physiological senses are receptive to them. Any change that is *measurable* is ruled by them. They are the absolute, standardized, dimensional mean of the function of our sensorial mechanism. This kind of time and space gives a sense of constant forwardness; constant non-variable passage that forms the basic properties of the matrix concerned. If we close our eyes to spatial things, a forward sense of our being exists that cannot (volitionally) be stopped or accelerated. Events fall successively, in an orderly manner, *towards* an end. Only through this kind of artificial projection can we bring forth into cognition the presence of this kind of time and space. They are both *unmoveable and unremoveable* and all cognition fits them *as if* they ruled all phenomenal happenings.

Thus, if we try to assess happenings in what we believe to be *one* single measure of this objective time (simultaneity), only *one* spatial objective cognition can be asserted, and a spatial cognitive succession is established. If only this type of time and space *universally* existed, then cognition would be a phenomenal piece-by-piece world. An artificial movie-like assessment of phenomena would lead us to a picture-like, piece-by-piece, inductive framework (phenomena itself) devoid of formative character or intuitional projection.

2. Variable time and space. These belong to the process we call

imagination. The constant forwardness is varied, by our will power, and the matrix operator concerned is characterized by these flexible attributes of time and space. It is intended that accelerations and de-accelerations of its temporal and spatial characters occur in order to define and re-define a situation. Time and space are varied *as if they were another pair of participating concepts* though they are the formative essence of that operator. They are manipulated as mere objects by the matrix involved to help determine a particular situation, in contrast to objective time and space that use the operator qualities to produce a cognition. They vary proportionally to objective time and space.

3. Positional time and space. These are strictly phenomenal qualities. They are the reverse of the previous two kinds of space and time discussed, for no matrix operator exists in *nature*. No forwardness or change in character is present although they might uncognitively form part of the intuitional process. Simultaneous happening defines this type of time and space; nature can assess a situation (even an infinite one) in *one* single measure of its time or accommodate all "cognitive space" in one measure of its space. They form the time and space properties of vectorial happening, of unending phenomena.

Positional time can be defined as a temporal like *a-directional* change; change that itself is without successive happening. It is the *instant* essence of any phenomenal event. Space is absolutely non-directional, time non-temporal. After their removal, a *no*-space-time situation would exist.

There are no defining boundaries present, and knowledge of the whole is a prerequisite for knowledge of the particular. And the particular leads to simultaneous knowledge of the whole. Eon or second, each can contain the same phenomenal event; an inch or the width of a galaxy, each can exist within the same absolute measure of positional time. Unity is variable and yet absolute.

Matriceal Cognitive Multiplication

It cannot be denied that when the mind is alert it is always conscious of something, meaning that at all times one of the components of the total mental function is at work. The remaining components of the cognitive framework are expectant and in a potential state, active even without the presence *in* them of a phenomenal happening. Intentionality can be claimed when we review the total experience of a long temporal act (from seconds to hours) and we recall this *total* form of a particular cognition that has continually filled objective time. But if we consider the absent state of cognition in which several of the operators were maintained, then consciousness as a whole was not intentional. What can be claimed is that the whole act of existing is intentional, but not the general act of consciousness that brings about that existence. To be passively aware of something by one of the modes of consciousness means that a reality has been imposed on us, that we cannot stop this particular cognitive mechanism, and that it will proceed automatically and end unvolitionally. This cognitive contest proceeds through a multiplicative type of inversion (matriceal inversion) in an all-or-none journey, and may come about through the confrontation with actual physical phenomena, imaginative phenomena (remembered phenomena) or through the phenomena of dreams.

Im and Con operators. The Im operator is the basic matrix originating *imaginary* reports. Its symbol.

$$\begin{pmatrix} - & e \\ t & - \end{pmatrix}$$

shows that its time and space are of the variable type (t,e). *It cannot produce imaginary sequences by itself.* That is a result of its interaction with the Con operator.

The Con operator is the basic operator originating *real* cognitive reports. Its symbol,

$$\begin{pmatrix} - & E \\ T & - \end{pmatrix}$$

shows that its time and space are objective in type (T,E). *It cannot produce consciousness by itself.* That is the result of its interaction with the Im operator.

34 INTRODUCTION TO PROJECTIVE COGNITION

Imagination and consciousness are produced when the Im and Con operators interact multiplicatively. Here we will only consider the Im and Con operators, for they alone can define a cognitive human being.

First cognitive proposition. Cognition occurs exclusively through a matriceal multiplicative process of the Im and Con operators. Vectoriality can be: phenomenal, imaginary or through dreams.

If

$$A = C_T^E = \begin{pmatrix} \overline{T} & E \\ & \underline{} \end{pmatrix} \quad \text{and} \quad B = I_t^e = \begin{pmatrix} \overline{t} & e \\ & \underline{} \end{pmatrix}$$

where C_T^E is the Con thematic field (operator) and I_t^e is the Im thematic field, we have,

Equation #11

$$AB = \begin{pmatrix} C_T^E \end{pmatrix} \begin{pmatrix} I_t^e \end{pmatrix} = \begin{pmatrix} \overline{T} & E \\ & \underline{} \end{pmatrix} \begin{pmatrix} \overline{t} & e \\ & \underline{} \end{pmatrix} = \begin{pmatrix} Et & \overline{} \\ \underline{} & Te \end{pmatrix}$$

Equation #12

$$BA = \begin{pmatrix} I_t^e \end{pmatrix} \begin{pmatrix} C_T^E \end{pmatrix} = \begin{pmatrix} \overline{t} & e \\ & \underline{} \end{pmatrix} \begin{pmatrix} \overline{T} & E \\ & \underline{} \end{pmatrix} = \begin{pmatrix} eT & \overline{} \\ \underline{} & tE \end{pmatrix}$$

Equations #11 and Equation #12 result in compound fields, present necessarily in the cognition of any reality, and they seem to be exclusive of the human mind. The product in Equation #12 represent a final cognitve concept. One of the most important characteristic of the above expressions is,

$AB = BA$ quantitatively, $\qquad AB \neq BA$ qualitatively.

This conforms with our previous conclusion that *reality apprehended (presented in a vectorial way by the world of phenomena, imaginative recalls, or dreams) suffers a qualitative matriceal inversion that progresses from vectorial apprehension into scalar cognition, following a U-turn back into the world that is now phenomenon.*

This is analogous to the mirror-like inversion encountered in Chapter 1.

Thematic Field Theory

Complete thematic field. As before, if we assume that

$$A = \left(\overline{\underline{T}} \ \underline{E}\right) \text{ and } B = \left(\overline{\underline{}} \ \underline{\underline{t}} \ \underline{e}\right)$$

and if r_0 is equal to vectorial phenomena, r_1 is equal to *unconscious* vectorial perception and r_2 is equal to scalar phenomenon, then we have,

Equation #13

$$r_1 \left(\overline{\underline{}} \ \underline{\underline{t}} \ \underline{e}\right)\left(\overline{\underline{T}} \ \underline{E}\right) \xrightarrow{} \text{Phenomena } (r_0)$$
$$\xrightarrow{} \text{Phenomena } (r_2)$$

which is a graphical example of Equations #11 and #12, page 34. Phenomena (r_0) and phenomenon (r_2) are almost instantly identified as the same thing. Phenomenon (r_2) is the result of a qualitative inversion of the phenomena into scalar conception, the only possible way for cognition.

Phenomena may come from stored cognitive sequences (imaginative recalls) or dreams, and not necessarily from the vectorial phenomenal world. As expressed before, r_2 gathers around itself a meaning posed by the self-indicativeness of scalar concepts, making the inversion necessary for the phenomenon of cognition.

Incomplete thematic fields. (a) The heterogenous type. If

$$A = \left(\overline{\underline{}} \ \underline{E}\right) \text{ and } B = \left(\overline{\underline{}} \ \underline{\underline{t}} \ \underline{}\right) \text{ then,}$$

Equation #14

$$AB = \left(\underline{Et} \ \underline{}\right) \text{ and } BA = \left(\overline{\underline{}} \ \overline{tE}\right)$$

and if

$$A = \left(\overline{\underline{T}} \ \underline{}\right) \text{ and } B = \left(\overline{\underline{}} \ \underline{e}\right) \text{ then}$$

Equation #15

$$AB = \begin{pmatrix} - & - \\ - & T_e \end{pmatrix} \text{ and } BA = \begin{pmatrix} eT & - \\ - & - \end{pmatrix}$$

We can see that

$AB = BA$ quantitatively and $AB \neq BA$ qualitatively

and we have the same results as in the complete thematic field.

In these examples A and B are important because they may exist as a variation of the respective complete matrices. It follows that a pure time or a pure space existence, if possible, can exist only as incomplete time-space matrices. We can say that to exist, heterogenous thematic fields must be required minimums.

Equation #15 defines variable space configuration in rigidly *progressing* time (objective time); it projects a fixed directional-temporal screen into variable configurational space. Equation #14 defines constant object configuration interacting in variable time; it projects fixed *demonstrative*-type objects into a test variable screen time. Then BA in Equation #15 plus BA in Equation #14 will give regular constant cognition as in Equation #12, page 34. The act of reason follows this additive pattern.

(b) The homogenous type. If

$$A = \begin{pmatrix} - & - \\ T & - \end{pmatrix} \text{ and } B = \begin{pmatrix} - & - \\ t & - \end{pmatrix}$$

then $AB = 0$ and $BA = 0$ and there is no cognition.

Disconnection

Equations #11 and #12, page 34, exemplify the main type of ordinary cognition; they represent the usual mode of alertness that alternates its existence with imaginary and dream-like alertness. During imaginary cognition the Con operator divides its function in two ways, (a) taking part in the imaginary cognitive inversion and (b) presenting a non-cognitive face to incoming phenomena. An example in (a) will be shortly discussed, and (b) can be represented graphically as follows,

Equation #16

$$r_0 \quad \boxed{\left(\dfrac{}{T}\dfrac{E}{}\right)} \begin{matrix} \leftarrow r_0 \\ \rightarrow r_0 \end{matrix} \qquad \text{where } r_0 \text{ is equal to phenomena.}$$

Here, r_0 *returns* intact back to phenomena without any cognition being attained. A typical example of this is when we become aware of the ticking of a clock *after it stops ticking but not before*. It means that the Con operator had been *disconnected* and, though it was sensorially alert, no cognition was possible until a change in the general scheme (the stopping of the sound) brought about a subsequent union with the Im operator. The Im operator could have been making other scalar realities, as we will see shortly. Actually, this is the only true connection (disconnection) possible between the absolute world of phenomena and the mind, ironically unobservable. Disconnection (cognitive in other than human species) occurs during daydreaming, where the Con operator is *disconnected* (but alert) and also making secondary imaginative scalar realities.

Imaginary Cognitive Inversion

Second cognitive proposition. Imagination occurs through a reverse matriceal multiplicative process of the Con and Im operators. The reality apprehended can be from *previous cognitive set-ups* or memorial phenomena.

Here we have,

Equation #17

$$BA = \begin{pmatrix} I^e_t \end{pmatrix} \begin{pmatrix} C^E_T \end{pmatrix} = \begin{pmatrix} \dfrac{}{t}\dfrac{e}{} \end{pmatrix} \begin{pmatrix} \dfrac{}{T}\dfrac{E}{} \end{pmatrix} = \begin{pmatrix} \dfrac{eT}{} \dfrac{}{tE} \end{pmatrix}$$

Equation #18

$$AB = \begin{pmatrix} C^E_T \end{pmatrix}\begin{pmatrix} I^e_t \end{pmatrix} = \begin{pmatrix} \dfrac{}{T}\dfrac{E}{} \end{pmatrix} \begin{pmatrix} \dfrac{}{t}\dfrac{e}{} \end{pmatrix} = \begin{pmatrix} \dfrac{Et}{} \dfrac{}{Te} \end{pmatrix}$$

where AB = BA quantitatively and AB ≠ BA qualitatively. Graphically it can be as follows,

Phenomena

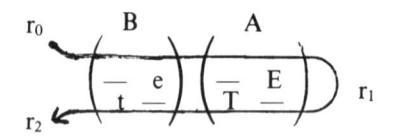

Phenomenon
(Imagination)

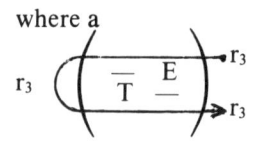

where a

exist at the same time.

Corollary to the second cognitive proposition. Intuition (intuitive cognitive inversion) occurs through a reverse matriceal multiplicative process of the Im operator and the In operator $\left(\overline{T} \; \dfrac{\Sigma}{\_}\right)$

where T (tau) and Σ (sigma) are its positional time and space. The Con operator remains disconnected and phenomena apprehended comes from Cv_1 as defined in Chapter 1.

We have,

Equation #19

$$\text{InIm} = \left(\text{In}_T^\Sigma\right)\left(I_t^e\right) = \left(\overline{T}\;\dfrac{\Sigma}{\_}\right)\left(\overline{t}\;\dfrac{e}{\_}\right) = \left(\dfrac{\Sigma t}{\_}\;\overline{Te}\right)$$

Equation #20

$$\text{ImIn} = \left(I_t^e\right)\left(\text{In}_T^\Sigma\right) = \left(\overline{t}\;\dfrac{e}{\_}\right)\left(\overline{T}\;\dfrac{\Sigma}{\_}\right) = \left(\dfrac{eT}{\_}\;\overline{t\Sigma}\right)$$

where InIm = ImIn quantitatively and InIm ≠ ImIn qualitatively. Graphically it can be as follows,

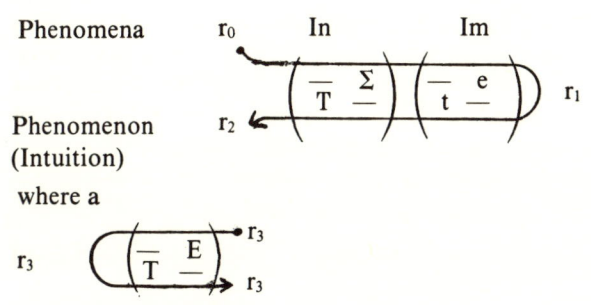

Phenomena r_0 In   Im
                  ⟨ T̄ Σ̱ ⟩⟨ t̄ ḛ ⟩ r_1
Phenomenon r_2
(Intuition)

where a

r_3 ⟨ T̄ Ḙ ⟩ → r_3
                    → r_3

exist at the same time.

The intuitive process is basically the same as that seen in imaginary cognitive inversion and has the same illustrative template matching as an imaginary process. If we close our eyes, the Im operator may substitute for the disconnected Con operator.

Compound Thematic Fields

The two products of the matriceal inversion in Equations #11 and #12, page 34, namely,

$$\left(\underline{Et} \quad \overline{Te}\right) \quad \text{and} \quad \left(\underline{eT} \quad \overline{tE}\right)$$

are a common twin approach to perception and cognition. They represent an already particular cognition, an accomplished phenomenon, not expectant operators. The second one can be equated to personal reality, heavy in scalar identity and emotion. The first one can be equated to an impersonal (non-cognitive) reality full of specificity, heavy in vectoriality typical of the first stage. Certainly error has no place in the first one, for it is the end product of a mechanism of factual report. Imagination, as the inverse of this general state of consciousness, reverses the role of these two products; but the same analysis applies, the second expression taking the place of the first and vice versa.

At this time we can see that none of them, without an inversion, can represent any mode of consciousness. One has to precede the other; a progression of both will produce scalarity that, after all, is a symbolic view or interpretation of a reality.

The combinations Te, tE are essential in the definition of any kind of cognition. The subjective variation of time and space observed or felt enables us to vary *speed* of physical action against a constant time reference. Thus one is able to speedily perform mentally using variable t as an inconstant scheme against a fixed screen of E. Equally, e allows presuppositions of space that against a fixed T give us *comparative*-type solutions to space problems.

Thematic Field Conversion

If we could define the phenomenal world as an absolute valued determinant, with a single, constant character, as in

$$\begin{vmatrix} a & \Sigma \\ T & b \end{vmatrix}$$

where a, b are fixed unique values and Σ and T are its space and time respectively, then a universal mind would see the same truth in

$$\begin{vmatrix} a & \Sigma \\ T & b \end{vmatrix}, \quad \begin{pmatrix} Et & - \\ - & Te \end{pmatrix} \quad \text{and} \quad \begin{pmatrix} eT & - \\ - & tE \end{pmatrix}.$$

If $\begin{pmatrix} - & E \\ T & - \end{pmatrix}$ is *strained* too far, it will fall into $\begin{pmatrix} - & e \\ t & - \end{pmatrix}$.

This will happen every time that we cannot maintain $\begin{pmatrix} - & E \\ T & - \end{pmatrix}$ within a cognitive *real* boundary. From then on, it is simply a repetition of the last cognitive (perceptible) boundary of $\begin{pmatrix} - & E \\ T & - \end{pmatrix}$. When we strain our awareness, it will fall into a repetitive imaginary view of the last $\begin{pmatrix} eT & - \\ - & tE \end{pmatrix}$ that is observed. This is the only way we can extrapolate awareness into the micro- and macrocosmos. If we could attain the universality present in an impossibly cognitive $\begin{vmatrix} a & \Sigma \\ T & b \end{vmatrix}$,

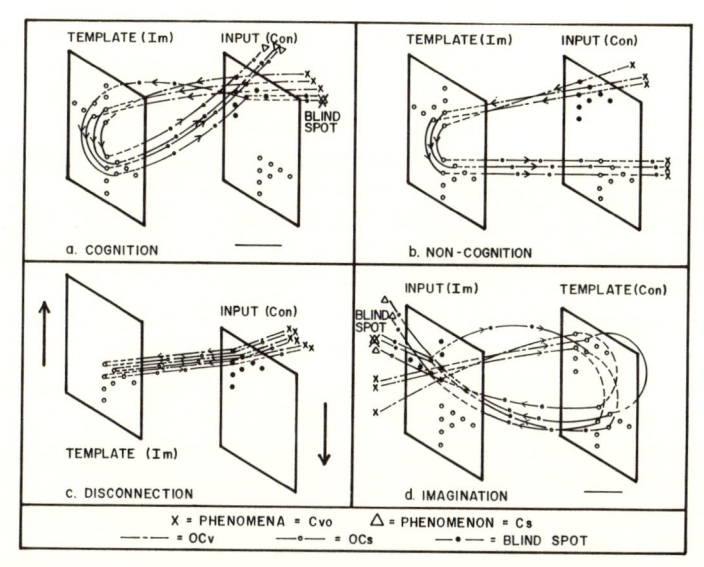

Figure 4. (a) Normal cognitive process describing the U-track travel back to phenomena. (b) Non-cognition at the apprehension of phenomena due to sensorial shortcomings. (c) Disconnection seen as a U-track back to phenomena but without inversion. (d) Imaginary cognition, where the Template and its Input reverse functions. This happens simultaneously with a disconnected process.

then $\left(\overline{}\, \dfrac{e}{\underline{}}\right)$ could not be functional, for everything possible could be contained in a cognitive $\left|\begin{smallmatrix} a & \Sigma \\ T & b \end{smallmatrix}\right|$

Reverse Template Matching

The graphical schemes seen in Figure 4 illustrate the processes we have discussed in the previous paragraphs. These processes alternate in an orderly way to give a smooth progression of cognition. In Figure 4 we note that:

1. Template scheme (a) represents the normal mode of cognition. The Con operator (input) pairs with the Im operator (template) to

invert, in this template, the cognitive path that returns to the input (Con operator) *as if* nothing in the individual concepts (dots and small circles representing the letter *A*) had changed through this pathway. Phenomena are represented by small marks (×) and phenomenon by delta signs (△). A blind spot is produced in the template where there is no right-to-left mirror-like inversion.

This template scheme alternates with template schemes (b), (c) and (d) and ends in either (b) (non-cognition) or (d) (imagination) through a disconnected process.

2. Template scheme (b) represents human non-cognition even when the sensorial mechanisms are functioning. An example of this would be non-cognition of neither the young lady or the old lady in Figure 3, page 23. A blind spot is not produced and the Con operator does not *transmit* the qualitative inversion. The unobservable confrontation with the macro- and microcosmos also belongs here.

3. Template scheme (c) represents the disconnected act. It is *as if* the operators (Con and Im) suffered a downward and upward displacement respectively to geometrically match their a priori setup (the letter *A* in this case). No inversion is seen and only blind spots are produced.

4. Template scheme (d) represents normal imaginary cognition which is only the reversal of template scheme (a). It is simultaneous with (c) and alternates with (a).

Chapter 3
The Inversive Phenomenon

Knowing as an Inversive Alternative

Cognition is a human alternative that does not conform with the purpose and reality of natural phenomena; the rigorous objective function devoid of self-observance characteristic of phenomenal happening does not admit the pre- or post-conceptual actualization (in the present "I") that defines cognition. It is an alternative that can give a trace-back, in an invariable way, to the reality of natural phenomena that creates the basic essence of existence. Since it is impossible for the human mind to *elucidate* such ways, an artificial system can be developed that satisfies as being an image of that unknown mechanism. To have assigned some kind of an undefined inversive act to this unknown mechanism (or mechanisms) usually results in an artificial cognitive framework that can give a tracing back to an understandable true reality of natural phenomena.

Here the following is proposed: that the matriceal inversion previously studied *is not* the final act of Logos by which cognition is attained. That the matriceal inversion is just another *result* of the mechanism by which this *Logos* exists and that we have used this inversion to exemplify the significance of this *Logos* in a mechanism that could be understood. If we remove the matriceal inversion as a general cognitive mechanism, retaining the principles that through this inversion we were able to recognize, then we have to accept the reality that inversiveness is a general cognitive law present in each cognitive phenomenon. Matriceal Algebra is one of the results of this. In the conception of all the physical laws that man has had the opportunity to assert, not a single example will be found in which inversiveness can not be traced as its cognitive nature. Typical examples of this, of which Matriceal Algebra, Eigenvalue problems, Functions of a Complex Variable, and Fourier Analysis are the most explicative, serve as an illustration of what the mind *is* and not of what it can produce.

An important observation of the above cognitive inversive assumption would be that *knowing is an inversive alternative, and all products of knowing proclaim an inversive nature*.

The inversive scheme assumed between man and nature studied in the previous chapters, is not *the* mental mechanism by which such an alternative comes to being, but it is only one way, in the manner of an example, that almost completely portrays the existence of a representative dynamics of mental function. What we know as the mind is an orderly collection of inversive alternative acts and whatever the *mind* produces is a two-part contrast between phenomena and brain *that never leaves the mind to affect phenomena again*.

Phenomena seem to exist behind every act of awareness that this mind is capable of achieving. Anything, even the awareness of the inner self, is the contemplation of external phenomena. All that can be substracted and *possessed* inversely in a cognition is *apart* from the cognitive entity, and belongs to the world of phenomena. The greater the abstraction in our own thinking the closer we come to self-cognitive destruction; and it seems that our own self is constantly generated, elusively hiding itself in the continuous stream of personal history.

The successive continuity that results when one form of cognitive inversion follows another (through the act of disconnection), produces a constant inversive state that makes us experience ourselves in a state of total intentional relationship with phenomena. But where lie those forms of awareness, dormant, *disconnected* while another form functions? They are part of a total non-intentional presence, expectant *and consuming its mental share of psychic energy in order to exist*. Every present moment sustains a personal Ego, and this is determined by a particular form of inversiveness that precludes, by the act of disconnection, other forms of cognitive inversion. The uneasiness that results from the passage of one form of inversiveness to another produces the *feeling* of particular meaning that enhances the *creation* of that particular Ego. The apparently vital character of every particular act of cognition belongs uniquely to each individual, as he becomes an essential being that refuses to be relegated in the face of this disturbing *switching* of the forms of awareness.

Positional happening leads the mind to the formation of inversive alternatives. Basic inversive alternatives are taken for *granted* by the inversive mind, achieving unattended passing through our awareness. The phenomenon of gravity is an example of such a basic alternative, inverted but *as if* in disconnection; we perceive all of its consequences, but not itself as a consequence. Thus, it remains untested as a recognized inversive alternative to the average individual. The concept of mass, the concept of movement are basic, constant unattended inversive alternatives.

On the other hand, the concept of energy (e.g., heat), the phenomenon of inertia, light, test their reality constantly, not falling in the category of basic inversive alternatives. The former inversion, being recognized almost always elicits in ourselves the angry frustration of an obvious thing that for long has eluded our discerning because of its *unfrictionless* passage through the mind mechanisms. While the latter does not need deductive work but rather passive feeling of its inversive passage through the same mechanism.

The complete inversive *product* of organized and pertinent remembrance that follows this inversive act is born simultaneously out of the same act. It serves as a phenomenal atmosphere for further inverse production. Creating a vectorial background out of the fleeting communion between the self and nature. It is to be understood that this inversion only pertains to spontaneous, unvolitive perception and is completely unaffected by behavior. Another difference in this category of (basic) cognitive inversions is that inversiveness that comes from phenomena whose phenomenon seems basic are accepted as a complete explanation of that phenomena. Their final, human consequences go no further than that of their cognitive initial creation. The understanding of the concept of mass holds no promises or perspectives to something beyond its initial cognition; it stands as a take-it-or-leave-it imposition. The search of further meaning is only a blank of mental work. The second kind of inversive alternative (passive feeling) is always easily understood, always pointing to the possibility of further explanation (as in the phenomenon of heat), because its immediate imposing of meaning spurs the mind on into further inversion.

We find in the principles of Functions of a Complex Variable an alternate mechanics that could have been used in the development of the inversive act. If $Z = X + iY$ and $W = U + iV$, Z could have been identified with phenomena and W could have been identified with phenomenon where $w = f(Z)$. The equivalent set of expressions $U(X,Y)$ and $V(X,Y)$ are real functions that could have been taken as a transformed image of specific phenomena values through the $W = f(Z)$ relation. The principles of Conformal Mapping would form an acceptable phenomena-phenomenon geometry.

The general idea behind these schemes is that all *mind* products can be traced back to some kind of an inversive act and that the most obvious forms (as in Matrix Algebra and Functions of a Complex Variable) are fundamental and can be used to *infer* the basic phenomena. Anything else that is perceived less obviously can be traced back inversely through different inversive patterns. The inversive act, in general, is the way to making a perceptive stimulus correspond in a special form to our awareness of such a stimulus. All that is human cognition can be reduced to a similar dual principle.

All cognitive process is an illustration of the mind before it is an explanation of phenomena. A mathematical idea, all phenomenon laws are examples of mental anatomy before they become an explanation of phenomenal mechanics. Merleau-Ponty is right in pointing out that every cognition that is taken as a representation of authentic phenomena has beforehand produced self-substance in anteriority to phenomenon truth. The old saying that *the knowledge of possibilities must precede that of actualities* is true only if we admit that those possibilities are nothing else but Ego substance that has been created in a *phenomenon-cognitive* run toward that actuality.

Graphical Principles of the Inversive Act

The phenomenon of cognition depends on a directional time-space lapse, contrary to phenomenal happening that exists on a positional-simultaneous *instant* of creation. The Geometrical Principles to be developed on this basis must have their beginning in such a positional-simultaneous character and end in a directional time-space scheme. The *human* link between these two can be any particular type of inversive method that the mind chooses to develop. As an example, let us analyze the simple Lyer-Müller visual comparison of two lines:

<------>   >------<

Actual cognition *leads* to the conclusion, in this instance, that only in artificial situations (as the one above) is one able to abstract an object (or one of its properties) from its surroundings (the difference in length between the two lines will disappear in a *real* multi-concept situation), since we are seldom aware, in actual situations, of the results of the above abstraction. But the mind follows the dual path of a Lyer-Müller mechanism where actual and artificial realities are separated into temporal compositions. It has been seen in previous examples that in actual situations some properties (as in *chair*) are relegated into vectoriality, thus making cognitively incomplete the actual phenomenal reports. In the Lyer-Müller scheme, the line in the right looks larger than the one in the left, even if we can attest that they are of equal length by *measuring* them. This is a case where instant phenomenal *perception* is needed to be able to assess the equality. The line at the right side is larger than the one in the left in a *time-space lapse* (visual comparison time); if we could, in a visual simultaneous way (outside a directional T-E lapse), make the comparison, the difference in length would disappear. When we make use of the ruler to test the visual report, *we are artificially making a positional-simultaneous background* out of the fixed space in the ruler. Hence the distance comes out to be *equal from one point of view (vectorial), and unequal from another point of view (scalar).* This analysis results in the following: (a) a cognitive act, where the lines are unequal, (b) an inversive scheme (the ruler) throughout which we trace back the phenomena, (c) the phenomenal act, where the lines are equal.

When we follow this type of *cognitive* path into the world of phenomena through an inversive mechanism, we can establish the principles of an Inversive Geometry based on this phenomena-phenomenon type of action. We will first define the cognitive blind spot found in all cognitive acts. Consider the XY plane. If to the $-X$, $+Y$ quadrant we assign phenomenal happening and to the $+X$, $+Y$ quadrant assign phenomenon happening, two possibilities will be considered that take the phenomenal act into the phenomenon quadrant. (a) *Phenomena* is transposed as it exists algebraically to the *phenomenon* quadrant; that is, Y retains its value as X changes its value (an unrotated *slide* of one quadrant over the other) or, (b) *phenomena* is transposed to the $+X$, $+Y$ quadrant by a 180° rotation over the Y axis.

On the first instance (a), cognition would be an exact view of phenomena seen with such accuracy as only nature herself can attain. It would be phenomena cognitive *as* phenomena in their very essence. The second (b) possibility is the *actual mind mechanism* where a rotational inversion takes place, phenomenon attained in an inverse relation to phenomena as it should be cognitive uninversely.

In Figure 5, page 49, the XY plane is used as a plane-reference coordinate site where *phenomena* are represented by a dashed line and phenomenon is represented by a solid line. In (a), Figure 5, on page 49, as X increases or decreases its value, Y retains its value correspondingly to those values before and after the slide. No cognition is produced here, hence quadrant values are cognitively ignored. In (b) the X and $-X$ semi-axes again coincide after the rotation. When we compare the result of this rotation with the result of the

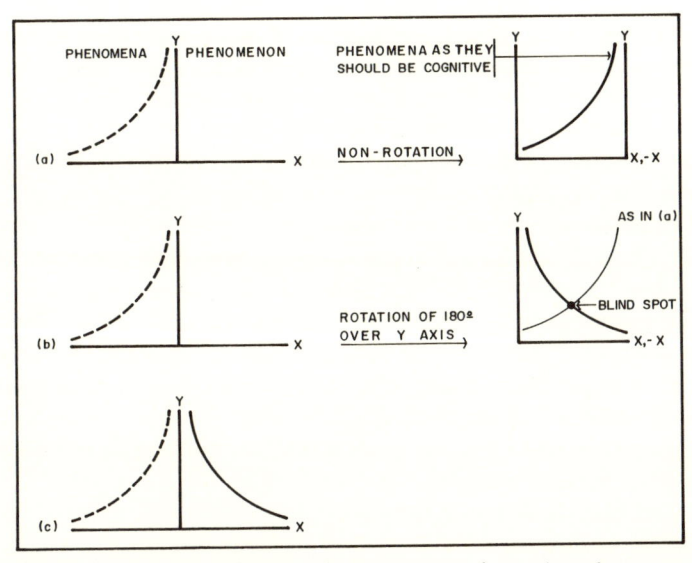

Figure 5. (a) *Translation* of phenomena into the phenomenon quadrant is seen, *as it should be cognitive.* (b) A rotation of 180° over the Y axis, with the production of a blind spot if cognition is meaningful and productive. (c) Phenomena and their inverted cognitive phenomenon.

translation in (a) (phenomena as they should be cognitive) then Y increases *and* decreases with a change in X. A qualitative inversive relation is obtained in the overlapping. This particular graphical illustration (b) represents one of the modes of *smallest* attainable cognition possible of particular phenomena; the intersection of the curves is at the farthest setting from a *zero angle*. This is shown because it is the simplest visual way that illustrates the inversion graphically. The greatest amount of possible cognition would be where the lines are *almost* coincidental (horizontal; cognition can be defined graphically as a progressive horizontal continuous stack-up of concepts); here, a *zero-degree angle* would be approached at the final inversion. Example: The awareness of a star gives only an infinitesimal fraction of the vectoriality involved in the total phenomenal being of the star (graphical case (b) belongs here) while aware-

50 INTRODUCTION TO PROJECTIVE COGNITION

ness of a light bulb gives a large fraction of the vectoriality involved. Here, the graphical representation pre-inversion is almost congruent to phenomenon representation post-inversion. In (c), Figure 5, we have a traced-back comparison between phenomenon as cognitive and phenomena as they are. The relation is an inverse one, for as X increases algebraically in value, phenomena values increase and phenomenon values decrease. In example (b), Figure 5, a common point exists where Y values are the same for both curves; this point, where the X and Y values are the same, is defined as a cognitive *blind spot* where phenomenon *intercepts* phenomena. The curves will never coincide geometrically for then there would be no cognition; they could *almost* coincide to the point of being coexistent parallels that meet, *creating* a zero-degree angle. Thus, one of the lines is either not straight in the sense that the other is, or does not possess the same properties as the other one.

Third cognitive proposition. A left-right inversive cognitive scheme of quadrants is attained at a 180° rotation of quadrants in the XY plane.

Fourth cognitive proposition. Common points of phenomenon-phenomena curves seen in the cognitive inversion denote blind spots for no true left-right perspective is attained in them. No cognition is possible at this point.

Corollary. If we define two functions, $Y = f(X)$ which equals phenomenon and $Y = f(-X)$ which equals phenomena, then we have

$f(X) - f(-X) \neq 0$.   Cognition is possible.
$f(X) - f(-X) = 0$.   Cognition is impossible.

Symmetry

Phenomenon symmetry (congruency) with phenomena cannot exist. If we assume that what we understand as symmetry of phenomenon to phenomena exists, then we would not be able to scalarize phenomena, for at all points $f(X) - f(-X) = 0$, assuming no additional displacement of the figures. Phenomena, in general, do not have the visual, rythmic, individual properties of the cognitive world, but possess *different qualities* from that experienced in phenomenon. Figure 6, below, is a graphical example of circular non-coincidental symmetry, where a *common locus* is equal to both phenomena as they should be cognitive, and phenomenon as cognitive. The concept of a circle, cognitively, has to be *marginal* from the phenomenal conceptual circle, otherwise there would be no cognition. But our concept of that circle is *almost* the same as that phenomenal conceptual circle.

We must assume that what we perceive as symmetric does not exist in the world of phenomena as such. Symmetry, identity, as we know it, are unrecognizable properties to nature itself; the more we *learn* in strictly ordered and symmetric cognition, the less close to phenomenal truth we are, and the more we need of redefining basic concepts. Schemes without common sense yield the greatest amount of understanding. The occurrence of a common blind spot assures us of some kind of perception; after that, perception proceeds as a personal act. The more *solid* our cognition appears to be, the farther away we are from phenomenal truth; the greater the percentage of unknowns, the more involved we are in a phenomenal issue. What corresponds in nature to our symmetric sense? Only by abstracting ourselves from the ways of perception and by using the path of an inversive principle as a tool, will we be able to answer such a question.

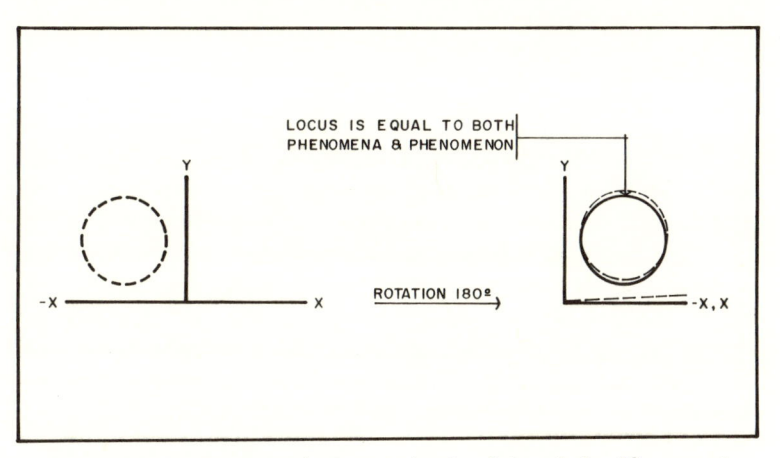

Figure 6. Non-symmetrical trace-back of the circle. If symmetry with phenomena exists, no cognition would be possible.

52 INTRODUCTION TO PROJECTIVE COGNITION

Fifth cognitive proposition. Cognition is always linked to phenomena by at least *one* blind spot.

All cognitive product, whatever it may be, always has some kind of invisible *link* with phenomena. The limits of awareness fall within an inverse proportion that is impossible to attain if a blind spot does not exist; if our senses cannot record, or the inversive contrast does not exist (with its blind spot), cognition will not occur. Even when our discerning cognitive mechanisms *can* understand, there cannot be a recognizable cognition.

We can see a geometrical example of this in Figure 7, page 53. The rotational result in this Figure cannot give any cognition, for no blind spot is produced; here, the Y axis is not coincident with the phenomenal Y' axis due to sensorial shortcomings. When cognitive rotation occurs, there is no point in common between the curves, hence no blind spot.

All knowledge that is gained through mechanical devices is valid in the same way that we recognize the workings of the sensorial apparatus as valid. If the final proportional contrast, with its blind spot, is produced through innumerable artificial devices, even then the recognizable cognition could be traced back to the basic phenomena *ignoring those artificial devices*, if for doing so we use the methods of the Inversive Principle.

Corollary to the Fifth proposition. Phenomena must exist to provide at least one blind spot.

Thus, a line segment, as cognitive to us *out of one single blind spot*, has an unrecognized counterpart in the phenomenal world that shares that blind spot with the human phenomenon, no matter how we came to the understanding of that knowledge. And it must be at an undefined *angle* since the phenomenon of the line segment is recognizable. If they coincide (*no* angle between them, which is different from a *zero* angle between them), a succession of further blind spots would give no cognition. Thus, a hyperbolic principle could be proposed out of the *single*-line-segment phenomenon and not as a result of a parallel line paradox, as is seen in the origins of non-Euclidean Geometry.

Sixth cognitive proposition. Cognition of a single line segment follows the act of inversion, whereupon a single blind spot marks the vertex of a zero degree angle *as if phenomena-phenomenon acts were parallel counterparts that have finally met at infinity.* (See Figure 9, page 61.)

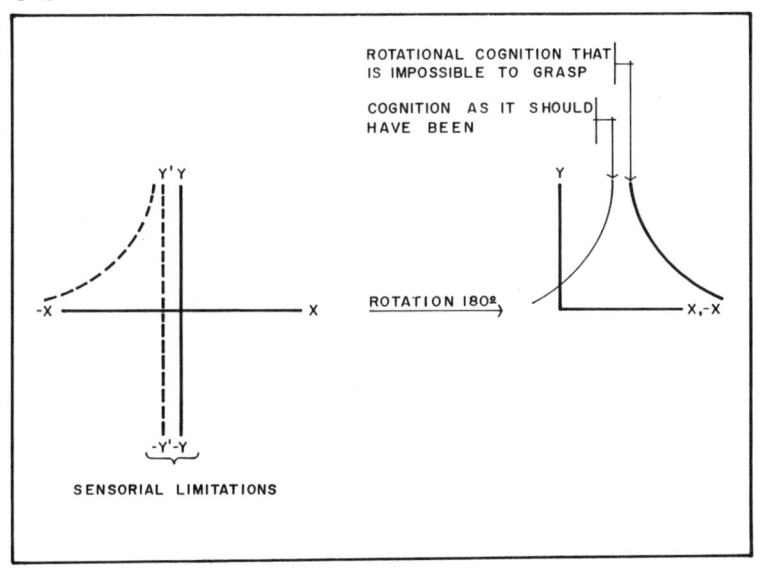

Figure 7. An absence of a blind spot excludes cognition, even if rotation occurs. Sensorial limitations displace the Y axis.

Continuity

If cognition is considered as arising from multiple blind-spot formation, continuity as we know it (the sense of solid extension) cannot exist as such in nature. If we assume that *continuous* phenomena exist naturally, then the inversion could not resolve itself in a cognitive way.

In Figure 8, page 54, blind spots would arise at all points after the inversion, without cognition being produced. If we consider phenomenon as coming from a horizontal stack-up (as described before) of concepts, *horizontal density* has to be less in either the phenomenal world or the phenomenon world, otherwise there would be a total and infinite formation of blind spots at the inversion. It must be assumed that phenomena which do arouse a phenomenon in ourselves are less continuous than the phenomenon they produce, for it projects in our minds a sensation of total solid extension. When a cognition of more than one blind spot is considered, the possible extension of phenomena has to be less continuous than the extensibility of a phenomenon to allow for such a cognitive phenomenon. Then, all properties of matter seem to lack the continuity of extension that we find in a phenomenon. The mind exists in a sensorial *bubble* of scalar concepts where *things* appear if in a darkroom under the guide of a focusing beam of light in which objects sporadically appear by the exclusive sensorial attention of the mind. The phenomenal concept of force, motion, when viewed under the Inverse Principle, becomes *porous*, less forcible and one step behind in apparent dis-

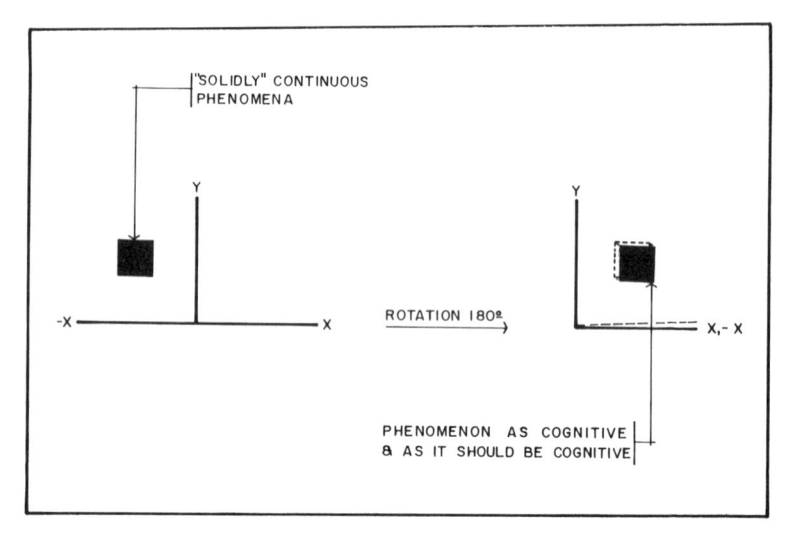

Figure 8. Totally continuous phenomena (*as the mind knows it*) are not possible, because phenomenon cannot be defined as a supercontinuous state. Cognition is incompatible with a universal formation of blind spots.

placement. *Phenomena must be defined as less continuous than the phenomenon they produce if perception and cognition are going to occur.* Phenomena, then, are less massive, less speedy, less energetic, less gravitational, less *real* than what they appear to be. Our mind weaves us in the above phenomena and magnifies their qualities so that we can engrave them with a meaning.

Most of human intellectual production so far is a mixture of mind experiencing its own mechanisms through the unfolding action of the inevitable phenomenal presence, and mind describing such experience as universal and final because it seems to last beyond its own temporal perspective.

Disconnection can be defined as a voluntary or unvoluntary denial of phenomenal continuity. Part (a), Figure 5, page 49, is a graphical representation of disconnection when no inversion takes place at a cognitive intent, as is also seen in Equation 16, page 37. Blind spots are produced at the *slide* displacement along the entire line because there has been no inversion, hence no angulation. Only *unattentive* observance is produced, where we participate in a *blind* attention upon which we cannot scalarize. Yet we remember it afterwards so it is somehow impressed in our memory.

Chapter 4
Uncertainty

The most distinct example of the Inverse Principle that can be found in the field of science is that of the phenomenon of Uncertainty as proposed by W.K. Heisenberg. Uncertainty is the inverse phenomenon in its purest form; one can follow its consequences through the act of cognition and state that Uncertainty is a phenomenon born out of the functions of the human mind, not out of physical phenomena. The following discussion develops this Uncertainty principle to its phenomena-phenomenon final conclusion; that it is a functional law of cognition and has nothing to do with phenomenal happening.

Max Planck states (*A Survey of Physical Theory*) that the whole range of Physics, its definitions as its entire structure, bears, in a certain sense, an *anthropomorphous* character. This suggests that the whole body of Physics is human-like, human oriented and not exclusively phenomenal. Furthermore, we can suppose that this statement concerning the character of the subject of Physics fails to be annoying to advancing phenomena. The Inverse Mind, painfully admitted, is ignored by the vectorial world. This surprising truth becomes evident because of the a-phenomenal disunity that inversiveness attaches to constant continuous phenomena which are oriented in an existence of perpetual non-order. Uncertainty clearly shows the kind of disunity that the phenomenal world cannot accept, for no such inverse disunion can exist in the same entity that *experiences* the dual character (observer and observed entity) of the phenomenon of Uncertainty. The object of the following discussion is to illustrate the human element of the Uncertainty formulas and to illustrate how the Inversive Principle can bring about solutions in the field of Psychology.

From the interaction of 0^- and Cv_0 indicated in the first chapter we can propose the following:

Seventh cognitive proposition. Equation #8, page 21, is a basic cognitive relation that gives the amount of attainable cognition against the amount of uncognitive perception in the AB inversion.

Since OCv_1 does not give rise to cognition (though it participates in perception) Equation #8, page 21, reduces itself *cognitively* to

Equation #21

$OCv = OCs$

All human cognition follows Equation #8, page 21, where OCv_1 is cognitively ignored, the process ending in Equation #21 as the only apparent *reality*. If we define OCv as a constant for any individual, e.g., $OCv = k$, where k is a constant, then we have:

Eighth cognitive proposition. $(OCv_1)(OCs) = k$ is a general uncertainty relation posed by the mechanisms of the mind into any phenomena-phenomenon inversion. All uncertainty relations must come from this Equation (Equation #9, page 21).

From Equation #9, page 21, two forms of uncertainty arise: (a) the one that sets an occurrence against one of its own properties (Heisenberg type) and (b) the one that is produced by setting an occurrence against an alternative of the same occurrence, both having the same and equal properties. The first one is called Quantitative Uncertainty, the second one Qualitative Uncertainty.

58 INTRODUCTION TO PROJECTIVE COGNITION

Quantitative Uncertainty

This type of uncertainty arises when we consider Equation #9, page 21, for its cognitive value only, ignoring OC_{V_1} cognitively, as we have seen in Equation #21, page 57. Then we have

Equation #22

$OCs = k$

that describes a Heisenberg type of uncertainty. If 0^- is defined as

Equation #23

$$0^- = \left(\overline{\frac{}{T}} \frac{E}{\_}\right) \left(\overline{\frac{}{t}} \frac{e}{\_}\right),$$

a relation results that defines an observer and we also have

$$\vec{0^-} = \left(\overline{\frac{}{T}} \frac{E}{\_}\right) \left(\overline{\frac{}{t}} \frac{e}{\_}\right) = \left(\frac{Et}{\_} \overline{\frac{}{Te}}\right)$$

as in $OC_{V_1}, \vec{0^-}$ the AB part of the matriceal multiplication, and

$$\overleftarrow{0^-} = \left(\overline{\frac{}{t}} \frac{e}{\_}\right) \left(\overline{\frac{}{T}} \frac{E}{\_}\right) = \left(\frac{eT}{\_} \overline{\frac{}{tE}}\right) = \left(\frac{e}{\_} \overline{E}\right) \left(\frac{T}{\_} \overline{t}\right)$$

as in $OCs, \overleftarrow{0^-}$ the BA part of the matriceal inversion. If OC_{V_1} is disregarded as non-cognitive (the AB or $\left(\frac{Et}{\_} \overline{\frac{}{Te}}\right)$ part of the cognitive inversion), then what remains of Equation #9, page 21, is Equation #22, page 58. This can be compared to a Heisenberg type of uncertainty by observing Equation #23 (BA part) page 58. Then

Equation #24

$$\left(\frac{\Delta e}{\_} \overline{\Delta E}\right) \Delta \bar{p} \cong k$$

$$\left(\frac{\Delta T}{\Delta t}\right) \Delta \bar{E} \cong k$$

where $\bar{p}$ and $\bar{E}$ are momentum and energy respectively. Cs, the phenomenon itself, can be equated to $\Delta\bar{p}$ or $\Delta\bar{E}$. Then Cs varies against one of its defining properties. The above happens in real or observed type of uncertainty when the time and space variables are given small (infinitesimal) values.

Qualitative Uncertainty

Qualitative Uncertainty arises when we consider the uncognitive part of Equation #9, page 21, OC_{V_1}. If $(OC_{V_1})(OCs) = k$ is considered inductively as a case of actual observation (OCs) against *possible* observation (OC_{V_1}) of the same phenomena-phenomenon route, then Qualitative Uncertainty can be defined. Here we have perceptive possibilities of phenomena making contrast with actual cognition of the same phenomena, not a phenomenon against one of its defining properties. It is a contrast of possible phenomenal cognition OC_{V_1}, against actual phenomenon OCs; a qualitative confrontation of phases within the same phenomena-mind happening, a contrast between an observable phenomenon against a possible alternative of the observance of such phenomena. When $(OC_{V_1})(OCs) = k$ is considered and OC_{V_1} is not *felt* varying against OCs (as is actually the case), the only cognitive real thing that we can be aware of is a quantitative variation within OCs, unlinked to any other inverse relation. But if an inverse varying uncognitive alternative is considered, then we could arrive at such a relation as $(OC_{V_1})(OCs) = k$.

In actual observance, there is a *liberal* relation of the factors involved in this qualitative type of uncertainty (between OC_{V_1} and OCs). Apprehension of the same phenomena differs in our minds from happening to happening in such a gross way that the OCs = k type of uncertainty is completely ignored as *fixed* and the appreciations of the *same* phenomenon are taken as a different phenomenon. Apprehensions of a phenomenon where gravity is considered give different mental measures of the force of such phenomenon (from no gravity at all to exaggerated weight proportions); differences in dis-

60 INTRODUCTION TO PROJECTIVE COGNITION

tance apprehensions can vary from fractions of an inch to miles in *different* spatial situations. In these cases OCs in error is the only available cognition present, varying (uncognitively) against what should have been the cognition (OCv_1), this inverse variation subject to an elusive constant. When an atomic phenomenon is described, the $OCv_1 OCs$ relation is fixed imaginatively (for experience has given us no alternatives of either OCv_1 or OCs; we have no previous recall to match sub-atomic unknowns) into a constant behavior, allowing then for the observation of the *supposedly* fixed OCs = k; hence we are aware of Quantitative Uncertainty. Then $OCv_1 OCs$ is an expression that measures everyday human error when its components follow an inverse variation. When an erratic Cs appears, then OCv_1 makes its presence *felt* at the moment of the mistaken Cs. This means that there is a constant erroneous awareness of phenomena with a *hint* brought about by OCv_1 of such an erroneous awareness. We are aware of the possibility of error but we do not have to account for it; this is a neat safety valve in the error of judgments.

Disconnected Type of Uncertainty

If we make use of the alternate Uncertainty expression $\overline{X}^2 \overline{p}^2 = K$, where $\overline{X}$ and $\overline{P}$ are *mean* values of space and momentum, then after considering Equation #23, page 58, we have

Equation #25

$$\left(\frac{e}{-} \overline{\overline{E}}\right)^2 \overline{p}^2 = K$$

where K is equivalent to k in a perceptive-cognitive way. But since $\left(\frac{e}{-} \overline{\overline{E}}\right)^2$ is equal to $(0^-)^2$ and $\overline{p}^2$ is equal to Cs^2, then we have

$$0^2 Cs^2 = K$$

or

$$(OCs)(OCs) = K.$$

Uncertainty 61

Comparing this last expression with Equation #9, page 21, we come to the conclusion that $OCs \eqsim OCv_1$ in this alternate Uncertainty expression and that $(OCs)^2 = K$ or $(OCv_1)^2 \eqsim K$ respectively. Since this means that AB and BA in the matriceal multiplication are approximately the same, we have to distinguish Equation #25, page 60, as another example of the phenomenon of Disconnection. The cognitive meaning of this last Equation can be seen as follows. When real cognitive *mean values* of space and momentum are considered in the Uncertainty formulas, disconnection may *omit* observance of any phenomenon involved. This does not happen when we consider the small (infinitesimal) values represented by $\triangle e$, $\triangle E$, $\triangle \bar{p}$, $\triangle \bar{E}$. The above description agrees with our definition of Qualitative Uncertainty (where OCv_1 is seen as a *possible* cognition, and the values of

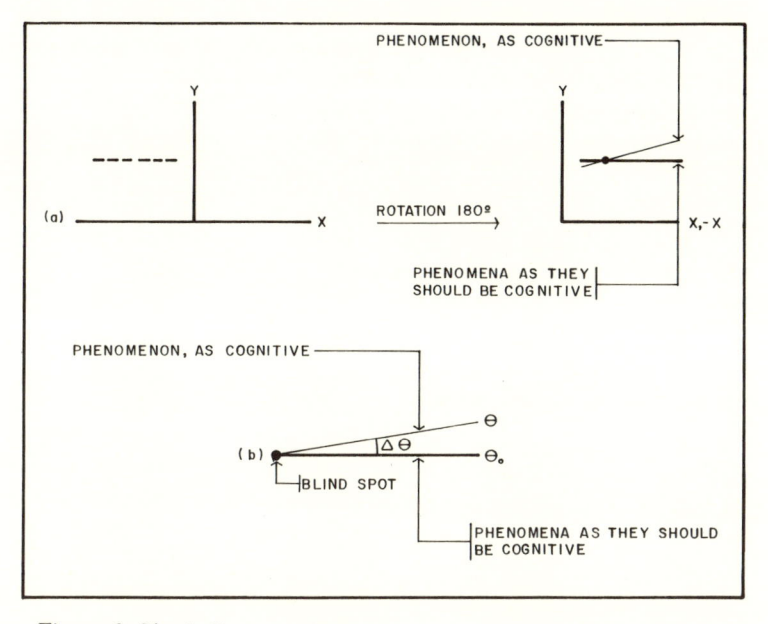

Figure 9. Single line cognition, as a rotational phenomenon, produces some kind of an angle contrary to the effect seen in Figure 7. This *zero* angle is produced *as if* phenomena and phenomenon were parallels that met at infinity.

the same phenomenon are usually unrelated, disconnected quantities) and Quantitative Uncertainty (where discreet values of space and momentum are considered *both* cognitively relevant).

Hyperbolism

The sixth cognitive proposition seen previously allows for the establishment of a Hyperbolic Cognitive principle. As an example let us consider the cognition of a single line segment; this phenomenon must make some kind of an angle with phenomena after the rotational inversion, for if coincident, no cognition is possible, as already explained.

Remembering that at least one blind spot is necessary for cognition, then we have $\triangle\theta$ (see Figure 9, page 61), a zero angle at which perception is established. This angle can be made to diminish within this *zero* dimension ending in perception (see *b*, Figure 9), but when θ *meets* θ_0 no perception is accomplished. This position defines an absolute zero coincident with the perceptive zero.

In (b) Figure 9, page 61, we have

θ = perceptive zero.
θ_0 = absolute unperceptive zero.
$\triangle\theta$ = zero angle (measures possible amount of cognition).

The above statements define a Hyperbolic Principle on the basis of a single line phenomenon, setting aside the parallel line paradox seen in non-Euclidean Geometry.

Chapter 5
Memory

Disconnection

The mind, in order to engage itself in one of the forms of memory (visual, auditive, etc.), must invariably disconnect its inversive consciousness; it must remain *unconsciously* aware of vectoriality while producing a *secondary* scalar inmediate reality. This form of disconnection has a time limit of seconds (or fractions of a second) similar to the time lapse of *icon* imagination, and follows the rules of the

disjunction (disconnection) previously studied where $\left(\dfrac{-}{T} \dfrac{E}{-} \right)$

remains passively vectorial and uncognitive.

This phenomenon is similar to a *disconnected memorial window* (see Figure 10, page 64) that opens inward (imaginatively) and closes outward to allow memorial recall. This memorial window is best observed when the act of reading is performed or during any sequential action where, while the memorial fact materializes (best observed with picture memory), we lose the content and the rhythm of the main conscious act and remain *unconsciously entranced* for an unnoticed fraction of a second while the memorial act takes place.

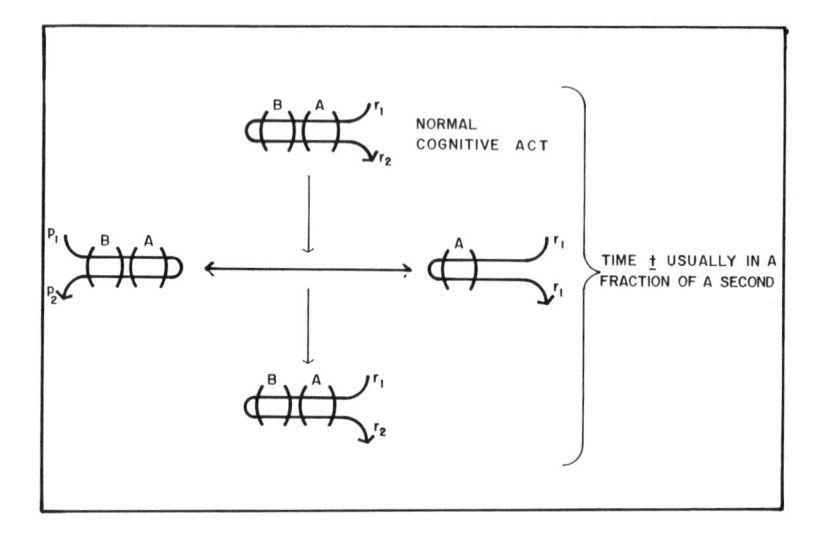

Figure 10. Disconnection is seen as a disunion of the Con operator from the normal cognitive act, allowing for a p_2 report. A *disconnected memorial window* is produced for a fraction of a second after which there is a return to the normal cognitive act.

This disconnected memorial window can be voluntary or involuntary; voluntarily it tends to be shorter in time but progressively frequent, while involuntarily it tends to be *deeper* but less repetitive. The strength and duration of this disconnected window is determined by the state of $\begin{smallmatrix}p_1\\p_2\end{smallmatrix}$ which represents an imaginary process where p_1 and p_2 are its phenomena and phenomenon respectively. This memorial window appears to be so profound at times that it makes us *blind* or dreamy to an extent where consciousness (at disconnection) is not functional.

Then a memorial T-E lapse can be defined as a disconnection where

Equation #26

Cognition ↔ Disconnected consciousness + Imagination

Imaginary phenomena as p_1 can be a previous $\left(\dfrac{Et}{-} \quad \overline{Te} \right)$ present in the mind as an uncognitive phenomenon. In this case it will go on as cognitive fact p_2 or it can stay as a stored memory p_2 after its cognition, producing a disconnected lapse called forgetfulness. An act of memory can not exist without a disconnected memorial window.

At times, when the disconnection affects the sense of vision, a reaccommodation of ocular function occurs at the resumption (after the act of a disconnected memorial window) of visual cognition. This can also be observed at the simultaneous sensorial touch by both hands, where we can feel involuntary changes in movement in one hand while we scalarize the sensorial data of the other one.

Ninth cognitive proposition. A recall intent, or act, occurs only during a disconnected memorial window.

Memory

The phenomenon process of recall or remembering has a time limit dependent on the time gap produced in its initial *fixing* disconnection. In general, impression time is equal to expression (or recall) time, meaning that the time it takes to fix a concept in a disconnected way is the time limit of the disconnection that requests the recall. A two-second disconnected time to fix six numerical digits will usually take a two-second disconnected time to recall the same number of digits. It can be seen that phenomenal concepts (vectorial concepts) are perceptively necessary to impress a significant memory mark, and their $\left(\dfrac{Et}{-}\ \overline{T_e}\right)$ are an essential retention factor.

Tenth cognitive proposition. Forgetfulness happens when the variable time and space content of $\left(\dfrac{Et}{-}\ \overline{T_e}\right)$ begins to fade away, producing dissociation changes in objective time and space and leaving the phenomenal concepts without Im time and space.

These phenomenal concepts may dissociate progressively, forcing $\left(\dfrac{Et}{-}\ \overline{T_e}\right)$ to disintegrate into passive absence. The act of recall or remembering is a single reposit of $\left(\dfrac{Et}{-}\ \overline{T_e}\right)$, this accomplished by the re-fixing of variable time and space into it.

Forgetfulness occurs, then, in three progressive stages:

(a) The t,e dimension is lost (variable part of $\left(\dfrac{Et}{-}\ \overline{T_e}\right)$ is lost).

(b) The general structure of phenomenal concepts is maintained (additional *fixing* disconnections may maintain $\left(\dfrac{Et}{-}\ \overline{T_e}\right)$.

(c) The general structure of concepts disappears, $\left(\dfrac{Et}{-}\ \overline{T_e}\right)$ is lost.

Recall occurs progressively as follows:

(a) The t,e dimension is added progressively to $\left(\dfrac{Et}{-}\ \overline{T_e}\right)$ in a correct way (this is the most common type of recall).

(b) The t,e dimension added is different from that lost. Here the *will structure* presents changed and bizarre recalls that are more meaningful to the individual, more convenient as proper recalls.

(c) Completely new erroneous recalls are produced at the failure of the correct recalls.

The following is a recall scheme that occurs constantly in daily life. Voluntary recall happens when we open, on command, a memorial disconnected window, while involuntary recall is the actual *physical re-living* (re-confrontation) of the act lost to forgetfulness. The following two alternatives arise.

1. *Voluntary recall.*
    (a) Remembrance of the whole act.
    (b) No remembrance.
2. *Involuntary recall.*
    (a) No remembrance. We may recall progressively *piece by piece* throughout the actual re-enactment of the original act. Actually, it turns out to be a new perception.
    (b) Remembrance. Here we choose to follow the re-enactment *piece by piece*, or we *anticipate ahead* of the presented scheme and remember correctly.

How could this explanation of forgetfulness fall in with our previous matrix scheme? If we consider the uninverted part of the inversive act, namely $\left(\underline{Et} \quad \overline{Te} \right)$ which could be defined as *unconscious cognition* very close to true phenomena, and assume that it has temporary properties at its imaginary t,e configuration, then we have

Equation #27

$$\left(\underline{Et} \quad \overline{Te} \right) \rightarrow \left(\underline{E} \quad \overline{T} \right)\left(\underline{t} \quad \overline{e} \right)$$

where

$$\left(\underline{t} \quad \overline{e} \right) \rightarrow \quad \text{disappears uncognitively}$$

and

$\left(\underline{\frac{E}{}} \overline{T}\right) \rightarrow \left(\!\!\left(\underline{\frac{E}{}} \overline{T}\right)\!\!\right)$ persists uncognitively in a disconnected form sustaining the phenomenal concepts.

In a similar way we have

Equation #28

$$\left(\underline{\frac{t}{}} \overline{e}\right)\left(\underline{\frac{E}{}} \overline{T}\right) \rightarrow \left(\underline{\frac{Et}{}} \overline{Te}\right)$$

which can be defined as a fixing equation.
Finally,

$$\left(\underline{\frac{Et}{}} \overline{Te}\right) \xrightarrow[\text{through}]{\text{B A} \atop (\;)(\;)} \text{cognitive remembrance.}$$

Equation #27, page 67, describes forgetfulness and Equation #28, page 68, describes remembrance. The recall factor $\left(\underline{\frac{t}{}} \overline{e}\right)$ will appear either by an act of the will, by re-enactment, or by both.

Backward Masking

Will a subject, in the process of learning two lessons, *cast* away part of the first lesson while learning the second? Or will forgetfulness be avoided by rest intervals between the two lessons? While studying the second lesson, the first lesson suffers forgetful deterioration (backward masking), but if a rest interval is inserted, the remembering score is higher than if no interval is permitted.

This could be explained, in the light of what has been discussed, as follows. The allowance of disconnection time, after a fact is perceived, permits a stronger permanent fixing of such a perception. Different lessons may need multiple (repeated) disconnected times throughout a lapse of minutes or hours to properly fix different perceptive difficulties. But even a single allowance of disconnection during a process of learning or memorizing will give a better end result than if no allowance of disconnection is permitted.

Disconnection allows for a fleeting reassessment of $\left(\underline{}^{t}\overline{}_{e}\right)$ *into the learned concepts.* During the process of learning a lesson (or in simple reading) we repeat this disconnection *inadvertently*; if an experiment is worked out to avoid this, backward masking will take place, and if the test does consider this factor, backward masking will be minimal.

If time is allowed after the final perception, giving opportunity for disconnection, backward masking will be progressively less. First items in a lesson are recalled more accurately than the last items in a test; this is so because the total time in a test gives better chances for repeated disconnections on the first items than the last. If the subjects in these experiments are allowed to recall in any order they please, they will try to recall the last items first, knowing intuitively that they have here a deficit in disconnection, and will leave for last the first ones that are rich in disconnections.

It has also been shown that if the duration time of briefly exposed recorded digits is reduced (but still remaining identifiable) so that the amount of time available between items is increased, fewer number of errors occur with such a compression in presentation. The longer the intervals between items, the longer will be the time allowed for disconnection, hence better recall after proper $\left(\underline{}^{t}\overline{}_{e}\right)$ fixing.

Eleventh cognitive proposition. A $\left(\underline{}^{t}\overline{}_{e}\right)$ *fixing* intent or act occurs only during a disconnected happening.

This fixing intent can be taken as an imaginative exercise or a disconnected memorial window.

70 INTRODUCTION TO PROJECTIVE COGNITION

Reading

There are three modes of reading, each of them obtained by a different process.

(a) The simplest form, which is actually non-reading, occurs when we visually scan through letters and sentences, with our perceptive mechanism in another cognition (daydreaming or imagining). Multiple disconnected happenings are maintained building a different scalar fantasy. Actually, there is no scalar setup of the material being read and poor memory remains after reading.

(b) The normal mode of reading in which the scalar formation of words or groups of words is obtained, scalar production being *in*

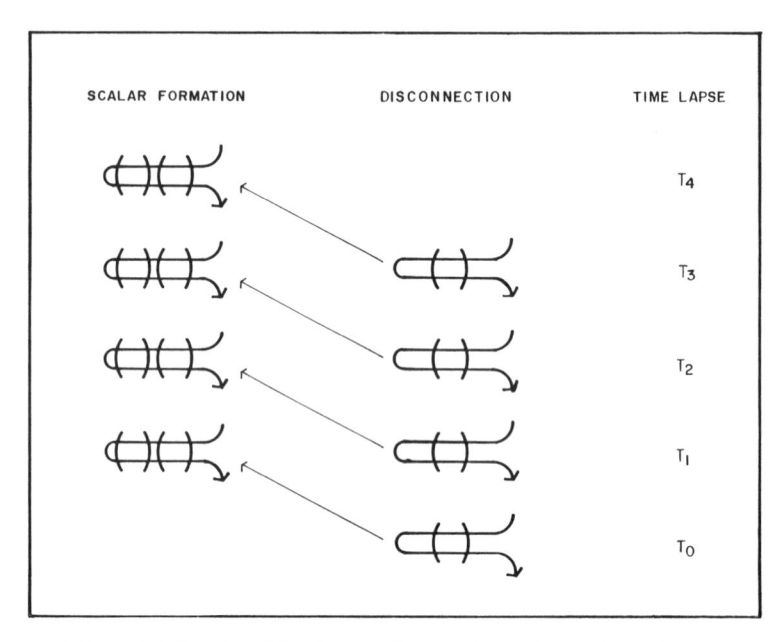

Figure 11. Scalar *delay* is seen in rapid reading, where the disconnected con operator is receiving actual data. A disconnection corresponding to a cognitive act is simultaneous in time with another cognitive act of a previous moment.

place (in situ). Usually the scalar-making process waits for the end of each visual fixing. There is good memory after this mode of reading.

(c) And the accelerated form of reading, in which at a time T_1 we scalarize the perception of the previous T_0. The disconnection *floats* at a present T whose substance is scalarized a fraction $T_0 - T_1$ afterwards.

In Figure 11, page 70, $T_2 - T_3$, $T_1 - T_2$, $T_0 - T_1$ is the time that the inverse mechanism takes to achieve scalar formation, this brought about by the *slowness of neural pathways and sensorial shortcomings*.

Process (c) could be equated reading through an *iconic* (briefly impressive) type of disconnection, while the one described in (b) above is a form of a fixing disconnection. It must be stated that disconnection is not an exclusive mechanism for scalar formation to take place, but it also allows for retention of that scalar fact. This type of a cognitive process is frequently found in auditory perception.

We can find an example of (b) in the analysis of the following *monogram*: Ⓐ, where an A is inscribed in a circle. To scalarize either A or the circle, we disconnect either the circle or A respectively. This is so for a fraction of a second and *in place*. We can find an example of (c) in the analysis of the same monogram, but now the displacement of time is so rapid that while we disconnect, scalar presence lags for a fraction of time behind its proper disconnection. The process is not *in place* any more. Thus in (b), disconnection is positional, in place, while in (c) the letter A follows the corresponding disconnected circle by a fraction of a second.

Chapter 6
Time and Space

Time

The Greek definition of time as a mobile image toward eternity is still valid; and the vision of eternity as immobile, where parts are not discernible, is one of the clearest and most important truths that man can ever envision. Only by understanding that what we call *time* is a union of duration (objective time), imagination (variable time) and simultaneity (positional time), will we be able to visualize the above definitions through the intricacies of modern logic. As already stated, time (in the commonly used sense) can be divided into three categories, but none of them existing by itself would ever give the human sense of historic time. They are:

a) T—exists as a measurable regularity, built into a mechanical human brain. It is here that the three modes of objective duration belong—permanency, succession and *cognitive* simultaneity. Mechanical devices, such as clocks, continually confirm this type of temporal activity and it is the one that we invariably try to describe as the total time phenomenon. It is also the one that we invariably reach with a clear vision and the one that is taken for granted in this type of discussion.

b) t—the variable-like type of time, residing in our inner sensibility, considered as an object by the *imaginary* operator. It is the product of a synthetic, malleable manipulation brought about by an accommodating, solely introspective operator.

c) τ—positional type of time that constitutes the simultaneity arising from a *contrary* T-t situation. It is the time of things-by-themselves (phenomena) where instant and eternity can hold the same finite or unending spatiality.

These three separate conceptions of time are roughly identified by philosophers throughout the history of man; but the recognition that time is a *cognitive* union, in every instance, of these three different a-conceptual temporal modes fails to come through in any existing philosophy. This privileged junction will not accept a separation inside the human skull, although, for the purpose of analysis, they can be viewed separately, always having in mind that each one is only a part of the total human temporal acquisition.

Bergson's example of positional time is most illustrative; the hands of the clock have no past or future and there is no happening achieved without an actual observer. The observer's eyes measure cognitive simultaneous acts between the pendulum and the hands of the clock, while to the clock itself only the present position exists; no past or future position of the hands is remembered or becomes in any way relevant. The past and the future have no meaning; all exists that can exist in a moment—a positional moment.

But let us imagine a clock in front of another clock; the actual existence of each of them would be acknowledged by the other as if this existence were an eternal (or simultaneous) happening. Now imagine that one of the clocks has an *imaginary* operator; then the objectiveness brought about by this operator (into τ) in the *now* sensorial happening of its eternal instant would cause two modes of awareness to rise:

1. A sense of succession from the present instant of actual objectiveness to a different instant of persistent objectiveness, this inherent in the variable constitution of the operator; and,

2. a *projection* (*cognitive* inversion) of the sense of succession towards the second clock, the first one *assuming* that the same objectiveness of the common instant exists in the apparently mirror

self-image of the second clock. Now imagine the two clocks contained in the same entity; here we have the creation of a *subject* that constantly recognizes itself temporally and eternally through the self-observation that results from the objectiveness that one positional instant projects into another.

Then, *instant* and *duration* can be defined as follows:

Instant. It is the self-contained feeling in which a particular *time-format* of introspective existence brings objectiveness into a *time-sequence* of introspective happening (as when the Im operator makes t,e time and space an object) through an *imaginary* type of mechanism in which the act of *existing* is brought forth from a dual positional state (as in the two clocks) where eternity is recognized in such an instant.

Duration. It is the maintenance of that singular (human) existence by a persistent phenomenal presence (that at all times acts *as if* the human existence were also phenomenal presence); thus continuity, non-repetitiveness and infinitude are present from the phenomenal side of the relation *as long as the other side (human existence) is present*.

It will be proposed that *to be*, it is necessary to be able to objectivize one mode of time into another. What we commonly call *time* is the instant production of the phenomenon of objectiveness (T,E by t,e in this case) brought about by a confrontation with τ, Σ.

Then the act of objectiveness is a state of the mind that prevents a positional assessment of things as they are. And from the phenomenal point of view anything else but simultaneity is a degeneration of the possible obtainable sense of positionality.

The further on we measure time by artificial means, the more *measurable* it becomes; the more we compare physicality with physicality, the more topological the mind becomes. The concept of duration grows into greater general terms than the concept of time itself and the order of succession tends towards the creation of a directional self. The measuring system becomes *the* system until the limits imposed by Uncertainty stop any further possibility of cognition.

The general phenomenon of displacement and the concept of time can be equated *cognitively* if we accept the following: Let us assume a bounded space as in A and B (Figure 12, page 75), with a variable X dimension where X is a function of the velocity from A to B. Let us assume that I is the phenomenon world of an observer (bounded in I) and II the phenomenal outlook outside such a world. If the world of the phenomenon observer in I is seen as a moveable leaflet world that increases or reduces its span from A to B depending on the velocity of displacement from A to B, then we have the following. If we insist in limiting the *concept* of velocity (displacement) to be constant as related to a seemingly fixed and universal *phenomenon* (light), as X diminishes (velocity from A to B increases, this observed from I and II), then space must suffer a change in its dimension (shorten) for we have conditioned the concept of velocity to a constant limiting extreme. Time must *slow* itself for the same reason (as already postulated in the Theory of Relativity).

We can see that a *phenomenal point of view* is needed to be able to postulate the space-time changes in the phenomenon world (I), *so that the observer in I can ignore these space-time changes*. If we allow X to approximate 0, we wil have attained a positional simultaneous situation where a positional type of space is now existent as time comes to a stop (reaches Σ).

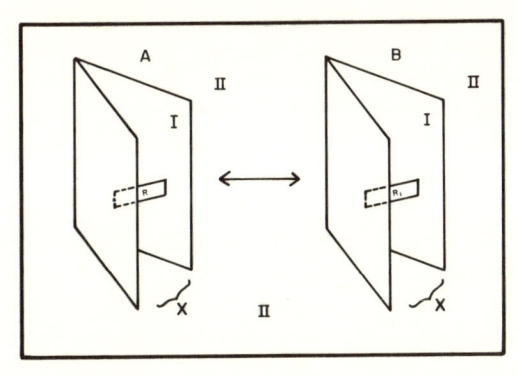

Figure 12. The distance r diminishes its length to r_1 because of an *external* velocity present from A to B, *this observed only from a phenomenal outlook* II that can detect such a change in view of a *totality* containing X. X will be seen invariant in I from A to B but variant from II. I represents the phenomenon world and II the phenomenal world.

If we take as the limit of X a positional phenomenal happening (e.g., the velocity of light is constant), X will vary its value throughout any change from A to B, *only from a positional (phenomenal) point of view*. The Theory of Relativity recognized phenomenality and assigned to the velocity of light the undertaking of such a measure (of X) and called this velocity *an invariable constant. The constancy of light is the first explicit admission of a phenomenal attribute in an observable physical quantity; it is the first excercise of the human mind as a phenomenal entity.* In any problem posed in this manner, the static entity (II) is always in a phenomenal position, maintaining a proportion between itself and the moving observer. Kant became a phenomenal entity when he postulated the singular properties of a judgment like "All bodies are extended." He recognized a *phenomenal identity* between body and extension (naming this an analytic process) while observing the variation between these two *concepts* (which are the same concept) brought about by a grammatical construction. When phenomena *observe* phenomena there is no need to proclaim constant concepts; the need would be to accept an inconstant phenomenon (I) that might sustain a change from the positional.

When we assume that the velocity of light is the first phenomenal observance by the mind (as phenomenality by itself), then we see that our conception of the world has to change to accept that fact. The *less solid postulate* of phenomenality discussed in Chapter 3, page 55, could have been taken as a form of relativity, for it allows the idea of contraction more easily.

This *less solid principle* allows the phenomenal world to follow this simple spatial rule,

a:a ↔ a

obtained from

a:b ↔ a

if we assume that the concept under consideration is repetitive. The idea of space will be developed from these relations.

Space

We can recognize two forms of type (b) vectors, as explained in Chapter 1, page 14; one that follows the way of cause and effect, this exemplifed by the general vector-scalar Equation #1, page 14,

:a:b: $\rightleftarrows$ a

:a:b: $\rightleftarrows$ b

and another that follows the way of the basic properties of matter that are *amenable to law*. This is exemplified by the following relation,

Equation #29

:a:a: $\rightleftarrows$ a

This can be seen as a special case of Equation #1, page 14. Equation #29 exemplifies every phenomenon that has as its essence a repetitive character.

A second illustrative form of Equation #29 is the following. If we consider A,A, a space-repetitive phenomenon and AA a corresponding vectorial continuum approaching a repetitive *positional* state, then

Equation #30

AA $\rightleftarrows$ A,A

where the left side of the equation can be taken *as if*, the A's were *shrinking and consolidating* themselves toward a simultaneous position, which agrees with the less solid principle stated previously.

This can be generalized to any vectorial continuum in the form of

AB $\rightleftarrows$ A,B

where A and B are different concepts.

78 INTRODUCTION TO PROJECTIVE COGNITION

We can safely propose that Equation #29, page 77, possesses the necessary philosophical conditions as to state it in a General Phenomenal Law that defines phenomenal space in terms of phenomenon space. Then any relation of the form

X:X = X

points somehow to a positional relation, originating exclusively from a phenomenon conceptual form. To reach vectoriality we have to include in ourselves the whole notion of a positional relation, this, if possible at all, through a relation equal to Equation #29, page 77.

To expand on this theme any further, we have to recall the sixth cognitive proposition (Chapter 3, page 53): "Cognition of a single line segment follows the act of inversion, whereupon a single blind spot marks the vertex of a zero-degree angle as if phenomena-phenomenon acts were parallel counterparts that have met at infinity." And if, as in Figure 9, page 61, and the section on Hyperbolism (Chapter 4, page 62), we define an angle θ as a perceptive zero, θ_0 as an absolute unperceptive zero and $\triangle\theta$ a zero angle that relates to a measure of possible cognition, then we can define a function δ that exemplifies the phenomenon of cognition as related to phenomena.

Twelfth cognitive proposition. The cognitive act and its inversive limits will be identified by a Dirac-like delta (δ) function where

$$\delta(\theta - \theta_0) = \begin{cases} \text{definable } 0 \ (\triangle\theta) \text{ if } \theta \neq \theta_0 \\ \text{definable } \infty \text{ if } \theta = \theta_0 \end{cases}$$

where θ_0 is equated to an absolute phenomenal positional simultaneity *similar* to the definable phenomenon 0.

Thus, $\delta(\theta - \theta_0)$ conforms in an expressive way to the basic process of cognition as derived geometrically from the inversive principles previously studied. *Space* is the presence, within the mind, of an eternal phenomenal assertion that is somehow discarded by the Ego in order to attain an alternate temporality, that, primordially, was determined to be a safe a-phenomenal world and more suitable to that Ego. An *involution* exists where the *place* of space-occupying-things reaches the limits of infinitude back toward the *place* of things-occupying-space present in the opposite angular site of such infinitude. Here is where the mind stands; at a junction where the end-point character of this placement will turn *dimensional* to a cognitive *anyone* that will not admit or will not recognize, at this site, the presence of eternity. Then, dimension is found at a conceptual infinity *present now* but unrecognized in the vicinity of this present state.

We can find an analogy between what we have defined as a vectorial repetitive continuum (Equation #29, page 77) and the delta function expression in the following manner: If in Equation #29, we substitute the Dirac function $\delta(\theta - \theta_0)$ (where θ is *vectorially* defined in a total way at θ_0) in place of a cognitive conceptual a, then we would have

Equation #31

$: \delta(\theta - \theta_0) : \delta(\theta - \theta_0) : \overrightarrow{\leftarrow} \delta(\theta - \theta_0)$

which conforms mathematically with the product of two Generalized Functions.

Equation #32

$\delta(\theta - \theta_0) \text{ o } \delta(\theta - \theta_0) = c\delta(\theta - \theta_0)$

if we identify the circular o product with vectorial coalition : and c with an arbitrary constant.

If we expand Equation #29, page 77, geometrically, then,

Equation #33

$:a:a:a: \ldots :a:^x = na$

where n is a number greater than unity (implying the additive character of scalar cognition) that has some kind of dependence with x, that is,

Equation #34

$n = f(x)$

where x is equal to the number of *coalitions* done in the process. Here x is a *phenomenal* expression that obeys the laws of algebraic exponents where p (algebraic exponent) is equal to $x + 1$.

If we expand Equation #32, page 79, geometrically, we have

Equation #35

$$\frac{1}{c^{x-1}} [\delta(\theta - \theta_0) \text{ o } \delta(\theta - \theta_0) \text{ o } .... \delta(\theta - \theta_0)^x] = c\,\delta(\theta - \theta_0)$$

if we assume that phenomenal coalition is similar to cognitive multiplication. Then we have

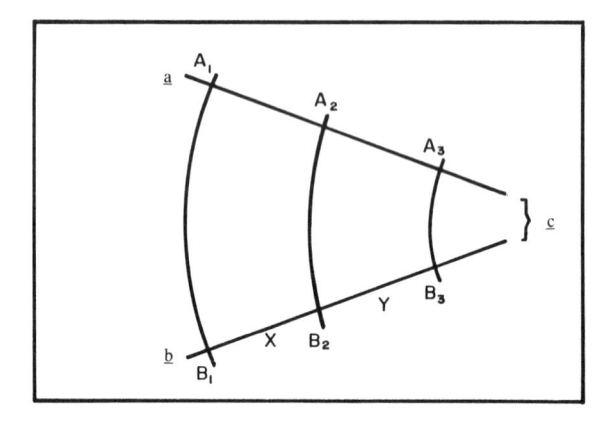

Figure 13. a and b are two parallel lines that meet at infinity c. A_1B_1, A_2B_2, A_3B_3 are concentric horocycles, and x, y are the corresponding distances along the parallel between the horocycles.

Equation #36

$$\delta(\theta - \theta_0) \circ \delta(\theta - \theta_0) \ldots\ldots \delta(\theta - \theta_0)^x = c^x \delta(\theta - \theta_0)$$

which yields

Equation #37

$$n = f(x) = c^x$$

after comparison with Equation #33, page 79.

It is worthwhile mentioning that the method for obtaining this same conclusion through the principle of the Law of Indices reverts to the same general expression of Equation #29, page 77. When figuring out the ratio of arcs of concentric horocycles (see Figure 13, page 80), if

$$\frac{A_1B_1}{A_2B_2} = f(x), \qquad \frac{A_2B_2}{A_3B_3} = f(y) \text{ and } \qquad \frac{A_1B_1}{A_3B_3} = f(x+y)$$

then

Equation #38

$$f(x+y) = f(x)f(y)$$

that leads to Equation #29, page 77, if we take x = y into an infinite relation. From Equation #38 we reach the same conclusion as before: $f(x) = c^x$.

Finally, we come to our last cognitive proposition.

Thirteenth cognitive proposition. The phenomenon world has non-Euclidean properties and is related to the phenomenal world by the expression $\delta(\theta - \theta_0)$, known as the Dirac delta function.

Corollary. θ_0 defines absolute unperceptive nothingness, *vectorially* related as a $\theta_0 = \theta_0\theta_0\theta_0 \ldots \theta_0^p$ continuum. In this way θ_0^p becomes a necessary perceptive expression that generates the perceptive θ.

Chapter 7
Perception

The assumptions that will be made in this chapter point to the fact that the phenomenal world could be exclusively Euclidean. And, as already stated, the phenomenon world could be unavoidably captive to non-Euclidean perceptive limitations. To sustain these assertions with new philosophical-scientific propositions we have to make use of the most accredited mathematical theories. But at the same time, rigorous mathematical formulation might, no matter how exact and seemingly necessary, render our metaphysical goals unclear. At times they might confuse intuitional truth that could lead us to genuine philosophical conclusions. Therefore, the mathematical structure to be used here will be subject at all times to philosophical propositions.

It might be inferred, by previous theory, that a scalar concept negates the essence of other scalar concepts, for they only point toward themselves. This is contrary to the idea of vector concepts that are always in continuous harmony with each other. From this, it seems that in order to reach the phenomenal world *we might have to ignore the scalar world and even discard, at times, common awareness.* We will have to rely more on our intuition than on actual cognitive necessary proof.

To advance these ideas into the world of phenomena, we have to adopt an aggressive philosophical attitude, aided only by an established mathematical framework. Here, we have to manipulate ideas philosophically and avoid falling into elaborate mathematical abstraction.

First, let us locate the Dirac-like delta function as philosophical data. To *be aware*, in the context of this function, is to maintain a regular correspondence with the world that surrounds us. That is, in a simple way, being is belonging.

The psychological act of being is that one where the "I" does not disappear in the presence of self-consciousness. The "I" remains aware of the self at all times and functions independently, depending on *no one* for its being. In the Generalized Function product

$$\delta\,\delta = c\,\delta$$

the term on the left side relies on phenomenal substance (existence) and simultaneous form (no dependency). The term on the right side implies psychological content (being) subordinated to personal space-time awareness. On the left side, content (δ) participates in the experience of itself (the second δ) to form an exclusive continuous world; it is the essence of existence itself. On the right side, content (single δ) is linked to an extraneous term c. This term makes δ dependent on something different from its being (δ). Its self-awareness does not depend on a second δ; it only maintains an undefined relation with this extraneous c.

This leads us into a position where we can visualize a Phenomenal Cosmology from a *perceptive* point of view. To improve on this idea we begin redefining the principles of Vector and Tensor Algebra. Using common tensor notation we have that, in general,

Equation #39

$$g_i^j = \delta_i^j$$

where g_i^j abbreviates the summation within the dummy indices j and i.

δ_i^j is the Kronecker delta symbol where

Equation #40

$$\delta_i^j = \begin{cases} 1 \text{ if } j = i \\ 0 \text{ if } j \neq i \end{cases}$$

This last expression is a fraternal variation of the Dirac-like delta function. One of its important properties is its relation to the contraction that might occur in a tensor. Tensor contraction always involves the appearance of δ_i^j. This makes us suspect that the contraction of tensors is somehow associated to phenomena-phenomenon processes, since a scalar factor is always produced when a dot product operates between two vectors and a δ_i^j appears.

These similarities are so appealing that we are tempted to follow the methods of Tensor Algebra and the unique property of contraction to seek for some link between the world of phenomena and the world of phenomenon. Let us try to apply this idea on the *perceptive* side of the phenomena-phenomenon mind route relations and see where it leads us. We have to emphasize that philosophical propositions will predominate over any mathematical considerations.

It was proposed that the phenomenal world is positional. Harmony, evenness of event, simultaneity form its character. The reduction of the large and the small to instant (positional) recognition has been identified with this phenomenality. The idea of infinity has no meaning beyond the human corneal barrier. Dimension and time can be reduced to a function of a phenomenal unity, its value or form unknown.

An interesting idea derived from previous propositions is that *phenomena cannot observe phenomena*. Since simultaneity gives to every form of phenomena the same view of an event from any set of imaginable coordinates to any other set of coordinates, the relation of observer to observer disappears. Then, no relative fact of anything against anything can exist within phenomenal observers. The appearance of relative events is only the product of a cognitive mind, and in the absence of at least two cognitive observers, there are no relative happenings. Then, to maintain the positionality of cause and effect, unity must be variable within the phenomenal world.

Second phenomenal proposition. The concept of unity is variable in the phenomenal world. The concept of unity is singular *and fixed* in the phenomenon world.

This means that unity has to be determined for every single event in the phenomenal world. We see, then, that relative *observations* of events do not exist in the phenomenal world and that the phenomenon sense of unity (singularity, one) participates *at some time* in the stream of phenomenal unities.

It is necessary that our goals be repeated: that we are *pretending* to reach phenomena through already stated phenomena-phenomenon principles and in the process describe perception in a mathematical way. These principles will be used at any time that is proper to advance our learning of the phenomenal or perceptive world.

Vector and Tensor Phenomenal Theory

In Vector and Tensor Algebra, contraction produces scalar entities. Perceptively, this means that contraction takes us *away* from vectoriality (or the phenomenal world). Since this contraction is produced by the special multiplication called the *dot product*, we have to do without this dot process if we are to advance toward the phenomenal world.

Third phenomenal proposition. The product $\delta\,\delta$ seen in Equation #32, Chapter Six, has the properties of a *dyad* as defined in Vector Algebra.

The dyadic nature of the association in δ δ characterizes the phenomenal continuum. This product is associated to cognition when x (the number of δ δ products) is equal to one (the dyad is a product of two vectors).

Corollary: The dot product, as defined in Vector Algebra, does not exist in the phenomenal world. It will apear only in the presence of a cognitive observer.

If a dot product (contraction) could take place in phenomena by itself, the Generalized Function (Equation #32) could not be used as a phenomena-phenomenon link. A contradiction could arise in which δ (dot) δ (scalar) would be equal to c δ (vector).

Beyond human perception (x greater than two) contraction *might* occur only in the presence of an Uncertain observer (not necessarily a cognitive one). Perception, at x equal to two, can be only intuitive and, at *some times*, the same as its pre-contractive phenomenal state. Also, *at times*, perceived intuitions (or cognitions) might not be phenomena by themselves. We can assume that tensor expansion could broaden the scope of a phenomenal happening. As an example, let us consider an expanded dyadic series of three vectors (x equal to two).

The Riemann-Christoffel Tensor

By exchanging the indices j,k in a triply covariant tensor, and subtracting one expression from the other, we obtain the Riemann-Christoffel Tensor (the R-C tensor from now on).

Equation #41

$$B_{ijk}^{\ \ l} = D_j \Gamma_{ki}^{\ l} - D_k \Gamma_{ji}^{\ l} + \Gamma_{ki}^{\ m} \Gamma_{jm}^{\ l} - \Gamma_{ji}^{\ m} \Gamma_{km}^{\ l}$$

Here, we have obtained a *differential inversion* in j and k in which the difference is not 0, or

Equation #42

$$U_{i,jk} - U_{i,kj} = u_l B_{ijk}^{\ \ l}$$

In Equation #41, Γ stands for Christoffel symbols of the second kind. The R-C tensor can be compared to a phenomena-phenomenon route present in this dimension of space.

Fourth phenomenal proposition. The R-C tensor is an expression of phenomenal state *linked* in some way to specific perceptions.

This makes perception, and not cognition, the end result we are seeking, even at x equal to one. We have to remember that perception is unconscious vectorial data.

Corollary. A possible perceptive act of the phenomenal fact contained in the *uncontracted* R-C tensor would bring about the highest form of intuition possible to the human mind.

This means that we have to deal with the uncontracted R-C tensor in the search for phenomena itself. A contracted form of this tensor would give partial or incomplete information regarding phenomena.

The Cosmological Perceptive Constant

If we suppose that the perceptive principles of Elliptic (Riemann) Geometry are equivalent to the cognitive significance of the thirteenth cognitive proposition and Equations #34 to Equations #37, then the principle of duality seen in this Geometry can be used to advance our theory. Here, the distance d between the poles of two lines (with an angle $\theta_0 - \theta$ between them) is given by

Equation #43

$$d = \frac{2q(\theta_0 - \theta)}{\pi}$$

Here $2(\theta_0 - \theta)$ can be taken as a *constant* angle if the lines are paratactic. If the unit of distance q is taken arbitrarily to be equal to one unit (cm, mm, etc.) and $2(\theta_0 - \theta)$ is substituted by K then we have

Equation #44

$$d = \frac{K \text{ unit}}{\pi}$$

where K is defined as a cosmological perceptive constant. or

Equation #45

$$d = \frac{K \text{ unit}}{\pi} = F(\theta_0)$$

where θ is equal to 0 from a cognitive point of view. But $\theta_0 = F(\theta_0) = \theta_0^p$ according to the corollary to the thirteenth cognitive proposition. If we persist in dictating cognitive propositions to perceptive expressions, then

Equation #46

$$F(\theta_0) = \theta_0^p = \theta_0^{x+1} = \theta_0^2 \qquad \text{at } x = 1$$

Then

Equation #47

$$\theta_0 = \left(\frac{K \text{ unit}}{\pi}\right)^{1/2}$$

where, by definition,

Equation #48

$$\triangle \theta_0 \approx \theta_0 = \left(\frac{K \text{ unit}}{\pi}\right)^{1/2}$$

where $\Delta\theta_0$ is measured in radians. It must be stated that Equation #44 could have been inferred from the third cognitive proposition and Figure 9.

If an undefined absolute valued $|\kappa|$ belongs to the phenomenal world and $|K|$ to the perceptive world then $|\kappa| = |K|$ would be a step toward the cognition of the unperceptive 0 (θ_0).

Geometry of the Sphere

If among the various forms of spherical symmetry we choose polar coordinates, where a line element can be defined as follows:

Equation #49

$$(ds)^2 = -e^\epsilon (dr)^2 - r^2 (d\theta)^2 - r^2 \sin^2\theta (d\phi)^2 + e^\zeta (dT)^2$$

and where we have chosen

$$q_{11} = -e^\epsilon,\ q_{44} = e^\zeta,\ q_{22} = -r^2,\ q_{33} = -r^2 \sin^2\theta$$

arbitrarily, ϵ and ζ functions of r to be determined, and the significant Christoffel symbols to be

Equation #50

$$\Gamma^1_{11} = \tfrac{1}{2}\epsilon^1 \quad \Gamma^2_{12} = \Gamma^2_{21} = \Gamma^3_{13} = \Gamma^3_{31} = \tfrac{1}{r}$$

$$\Gamma^4_{14} = \tfrac{1}{2}\zeta^1 \quad \Gamma^1_{22} = -re^{-\epsilon} \quad \Gamma^3_{23} = \cot\theta \quad \Gamma^1_{44} = \tfrac{1}{2} e^{\zeta-\epsilon}\zeta^1$$

$$\Gamma^1_{33} = -re^{-\epsilon}\sin^2\theta \quad \Gamma^2_{33} = -\sin\theta\cos\theta$$

where the superscripts indicate differentiation with respect to r, then we can proceed productively towards our goal of defining perception where r and T are now undefined functions of Σ and τ.

90 INTRODUCTION TO PROJECTIVE COGNITION

From the equations that result from the R-C tensor using Equation #50, several mathematical expressions arise. We will limit ourselves in this discussion to one,

Equation #51

$$\beta\,{}^{1}_{212} = \frac{1}{2}\, re^{-\epsilon}\epsilon^{1}$$

If we make the hypothetical statement that x as already defined determines some type of perception, then

Equation #52

$x = 1$ defines *real* perception
$x = 2$ defines *intuitive* perception
$x = -1$ defines *imaginary* perception

in an observer subject to the consequences of Equation #51. Furthermore, all cognitive propositions are valid within this observer. Self-evident cognitions (at $X = 1$) are *external* in origin contrary to intuition and imagination that are *internal* in origin. It will be assumed that mathematically x is real (equal to one) and consequently, a constant. In the discussion to come, x will assume all values listed above, but from a mathematical point of view x equal to 2 and -1 will be *cognitively* undefined.

If B^{1}_{212} is taken as a measure of phenomena somehow associated to perception, then, by Equation #9, Chapter 1, and the eighth cognitive proposition $[(OCv_1)(OCs) = k$, where $k = 1$ to impose *cognitive singularity* to perception],

Equation #53

$$\frac{1}{2}\, re^{-\epsilon}\epsilon^{1} = \frac{1}{x}$$

where Equation #51 is equivalent to OCv_1 and x is equivalent to OCs.

If we make use of the substitution

Equation #54

$$e^\epsilon = \frac{1}{\lambda}$$

where $\lambda = f(r)$, then we can solve Equation #53 perceptively. After a few mathematical steps we have

Equation #55

$$-x\lambda = 2 \log r + \text{constant}$$

This constant is part of the phenomenal-positional world. Then,

Equation #56

$$\lambda = \log \left(|\kappa|r \right)^{-2/x}$$

appears where the constant is now $2 \log |\kappa|$. $|\kappa|$ is defined as a *phenomenal cosmological constant*. In this equation, phenomena will be acted upon by cognitive ways (cognitive propositions) to yield perceptive data.

In order to proceed with our analysis, the following Postulates are necessary:

1) x can not be equal to a *cognitive* 0 (zero), otherwise we would have an undefined expression in the right side of Equation #53. But x equal to a *phenomenal* 0 (zero) could be possible.

2) In the spirit of our perceptive search, λ will be given the following meaning,

Equation #57

$$\lambda \begin{cases} = 1 \text{ if real } f(x) = x \\ < 1 \text{ if real } f(x) = e^{\frac{x}{Q}} \end{cases}$$

This postulate determines *types* of perception in the following mathematical derivations. Fittingly, Equation #57 represents a modified Kronecker or Dirac-like delta function where Q = 1 points to constant curvature. The term λ epitomizes perception *in general*, the upper and lower parts generating *operators* as defined in Chapter 2. The lower alternative will generate a type of non-Euclidean *perception* according to Equation #37, Chapter 6. Here,

Equation #58

$$f(x) = c^x = e^{\frac{x}{Q}}$$

It will become clear that the assumptions contained in Equation #57 express perceptive patterns that are not, in their totality, necessarily human.

3) Finite defined space will be a special case of perceptively circumscribed positionality where relations will have constant curvature.

4) By inspection, it will be postulated that a possible solution to Equation #56 is of the form

Equation #59

$$\left(|\kappa|r\right)^{-1/x} = e^{2^{-f(x)}}$$

this satisfying what is expressed in Equation #57. It will also provide uniformity in the formulation of the mathematical operators (m-operators). (See Appendix)

From the upper part of Equation #57, and making use of Equation #59, an m-operator solution to Equation #56 would be,

Equation #60

$$\left(|\kappa|r\right)^{-1/x} = e^{2^{-x}}$$

Equation #61

$$|\kappa|^{-1/x} = r^{1/x} e^{2^{-x}}$$

This yields $\lambda = 1$ when $f(x) = x = 1$ according to Equation #52. If we assign to both sides of Equation #61 the properties of an operator as defined in Chapter 2 and make use of the assumptions of Equations #52 and Equation #57, then we have

Equation #62

a) $|\kappa|^{-1} = re^{1/2}$ CON OPERATOR when x = 1.

b) $|\kappa| = r^{-1}e^{2}$ IM OPERATOR when x = −1.

c) $|\kappa|^{-1/2} = r^{1/2} e^{1/4}$ IN OPERATOR when x = 2.

$\lambda = 1$ can be attained only by substituting $\left(|\kappa|r\right)^{-1} = e^{1/2}$

in Equation #60. This means that "cognition" ($\lambda = 1$) could only exist as the production of a single Con operator. This suggests some species other than human in which the Im or In operator might not have been developed. If we proceed to other *psychological* possibilities using the (Im)(Con) and the (Im)(In) inversion defined in Chapter 2, we have (see Scheme 1)

a) $(\text{Im})(\text{Con}) = |\kappa|^{-1}|\kappa| = rr^{-1} e^{1/2} \; e^{2}$

The result is an inequality. Here, we assume that cognition, through this perceptive operator, is not possible.

b) $(\text{Im})(\text{In}) = |\kappa| |\kappa|^{-1/2} = r^{-1} r^{1/2} e^{2} e^{1/4}$

or

Equation #63

$$|\kappa|^{1/2} = r^{-1/2} e^{2.25}$$

94 INTRODUCTION TO PROJECTIVE COGNITION

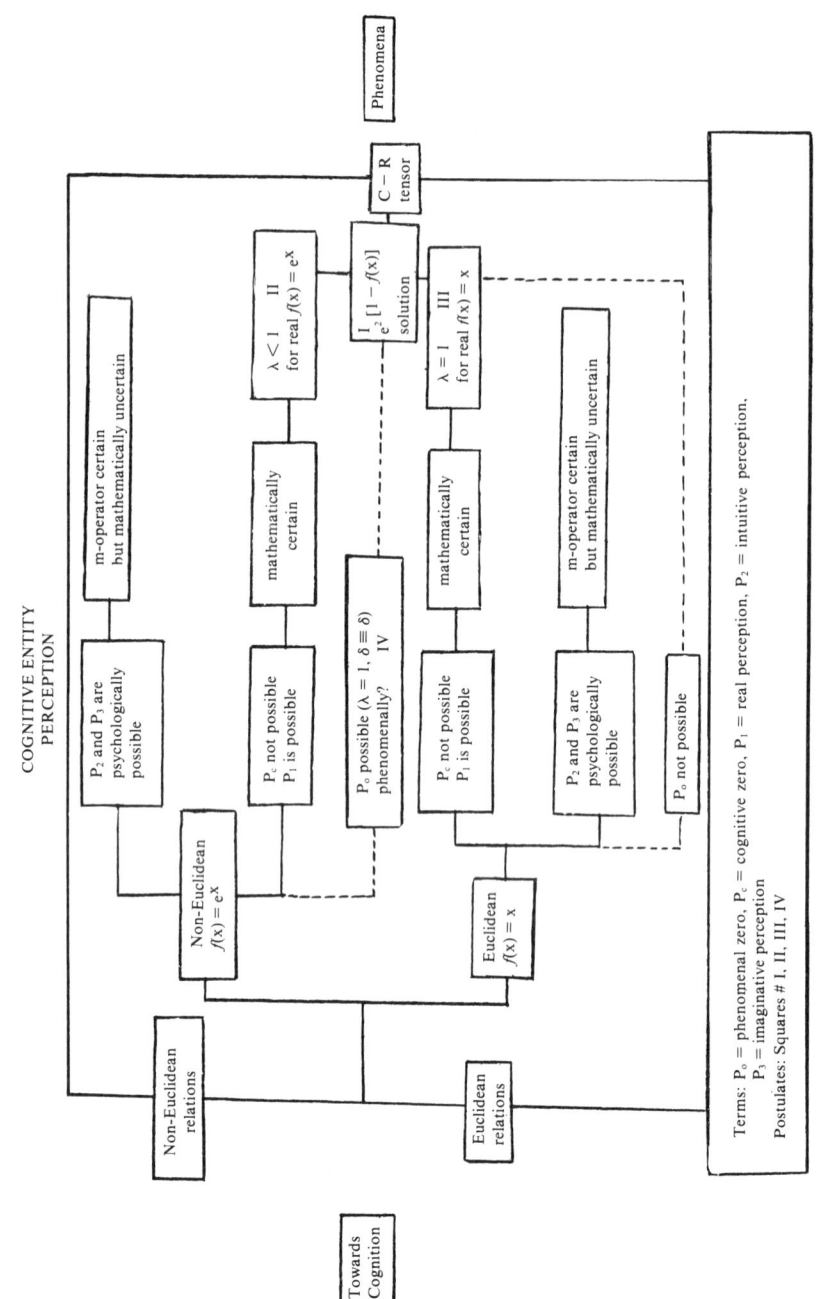

(SCHEME 1)
COGNITIVE ENTITY
PERCEPTION

```
                                        ┌─────────────┐
                                        │  Phenomena  │
                                        └──────┬──────┘
                                               │
                                        ┌──────┴──────┐
                                        │    C – R    │
                                        │   tensor    │
                                        └──────┬──────┘
                                               │
                              ┌────────────────┼────────────────┐
                              │                                 │
                     ┌────────┴────────┐              ┌─────────┴─────────┐
                     │   λ < 1     II  │              │   λ = 1     III   │
                     │ for real f(x)=eˣ│              │ for real f(x) = x │
                     └────────┬────────┘              └─────────┬─────────┘
                              │                                 │
                     ┌────────┴────────┐              ┌─────────┴─────────┐
                     │ mathematically  │              │  mathematically   │
                     │    certain      │              │     certain       │
                     └────────┬────────┘              └─────────┬─────────┘
                              │                                 │
                     ┌────────┴────────┐              ┌─────────┴─────────┐
                     │ Pc not possible │              │  Pc not possible  │
                     │ P1 is possible  │              │  P1 is possible   │
                     └─────────────────┘              └───────────────────┘
```

Square II: $e^{2}[1 - f(x)]$ solution

Square IV: P_0 possible ($\lambda = 1, \delta \equiv \delta$) phenomenally?

- m-operator certain but mathematically uncertain
- P_2 and P_3 are psychologically possible
- Non-Euclidean $f(x) = e^x$
- Euclidean $f(x) = x$
- P_0 not possible

Non-Euclidean relations

Euclidean relations

Towards Cognition

Terms: P_o = phenomenal zero, P_c = cognitive zero, P_1 = real perception, P_2 = intuitive perception.
P_3 = imaginative perception
Postulates: Squares # I, II, III, IV

Here, perceptive intuition (upper part of Equation #57) could be possible. An important consideration we have to mention is that $f(x) = x$ cannot be a human form of cognition (see Equation #36; $f(x) = e^x$ is the correct expression here). This suggests that the upper part of Equation #57 is not a human-type perceptive product, as already mentioned.

If the (Im)(Con) multiplication produces an inequality, then only the Con, the Im or the In operators could exist singly here. We choose to think that only the Con (and possibly the In) operator exists singly and that the Im is absent altogether, as might be the case with a subhuman species. The single (disconnected) operator could, possibly, produce a cognitive "piece-by-piece" phenomenon world in this species. If we assume that the Im operator exists, then the relation expressed in Equation #63 might be valid and its implications would have to be considered in a perceptive way. If the Con operator and In operators are the only ones to exist, then we can understand the psychological makeup of this lower species more easily. If the Im operator exists in them, spherical symmetry, intuitively, would suffer the changes in Table #1 (which would have to undergo a subsequent "leak" to be cognitive).

If we now consider the lower part of Equation #57, where $f(x) = e^x$, then we have arrived at the consequences of Equation #36. Any kind of perception that can be obtained here is human. We must state that x = cognitive 0 is excluded in both parts of Equation #57 by virtue of the first postulate. But the possibility of x = phenomenal 0 allows the existence (see Equation #36) of $f(x) = e^{x/Q}$ perceptively. From the lower part of Equation #57 and using Equation #59, then,

Equation #63(a)

$$\left(|\kappa|r\right)^{-1/x} = e^{2-e^{x/Q}}$$

the remaining m-operator solution to Equation #56. Here, $\lambda = 1$ is not *cognitively* allowed, for x cannot be equal to a cognitive 0 (zero), as stated in the first postulate. The alternative $x = 1$ results in an inequality in the (Im)(Com) relation excluding straight cognition. Con, In, or the Im operators could exist singly (as in disconnection)

96 INTRODUCTION TO PROJECTIVE COGNITION

as we know they do in humans. Another psychological possibility could be the (Im)(In) relation (similar to Equation #63). The existence of a phenomenal 0 (zero) sustains the m-operator fact of Equation #63$_{(a)}$ as a solution to Equation #56, for this allows a phenomenal ?$\lambda = 1$ and $\delta \equiv \delta$.

Equation #63$_{(a)}$ can be simplified

Equation #64

$$|\kappa|^{-1/x} = r^{1/x} e^{2.-e^x}$$

and we define this expression as the *Perceptive Phenomenal Intuitive Equation*.

Using Equations #52 and Equation #64 we have, then, as in Equation #62, where $x = -1, 2$ define psychological alternatives,

Equation #65

a) $|\kappa|^{-1} = r\, e^{2-e}$ CON OPERATOR when $x = 1$.

b) $|\kappa| = r^{-1}\, e^{2-e^{-1}}$ IM OPERATOR when $x = -1$.

c) $|\kappa|^{-½} = r^{½} e^{2-e^2}$ IN OPERATOR when $x = 2$.

representing an artificial perceptive observer.

The (Im)(In) alternative left would be

Equation #66

$$|\kappa|^{½} = r^{-½} e^{2-e^{-1}}\, e^{2-e^2} = r^{-½} e^B$$

where $B = 2^{-e^{-1}} + 2^{-e^2}$

Using Equation #48 where the assumption $|\kappa| = |\check{\kappa}|$ might lead to cognition (see Equation #46), Equations #63 and #66 could be expressed as

Equations #67

a) $\Delta\theta_{o_1} = \left(|r|\,\pi\right)^{-\frac{1}{2}} e^{2.25}$

b) $\Delta\theta_{o_2} = \left(|r|\,\pi\right)^{-\frac{1}{2}} e^{B}$

respectively (see Scheme 2). These Equations represent special geometrical intuitional perceptions that can be attained by one or another living thing. Table #1 shows examples in geometrical observations obtained from them.

Projecting the changes $\left(\dfrac{\Delta\theta}{\Delta T}\right)$ that would be observed in these "orbits" with radius *r* in one earth century, we would see an advance in a slice of their path ("theoretically" circular in this case) according to the results shown in Table #2.

Since *q* in Equation #43 may have any dimension, point and line are interchangeable as seen also in Elliptic Geometry.

If we assume *q* in Equation #43 to be one and π respectively, then at an $r = 6.96 \times 10^{10}$ cm we would have the results shown in Table #3.

The non-Euclidean unit for intuitive perception varies from one to π as in Table #3, or from *C* (circumference) equal to infinity and *D* (diameter) equal to infinity to *C* finite and *D* finite. This can be expressed as follows.

Equation #68

$$q = \lim_{\substack{C \to \infty \\ D \to \infty}} (C, D) = 1 \text{ unit.}$$

$$q = \lim_{\substack{C \to a \\ D \to b}} (C, D) = \pi \text{ unit.}$$

a and b finite expression.

98 INTRODUCTION TO PROJECTIVE COGNITION

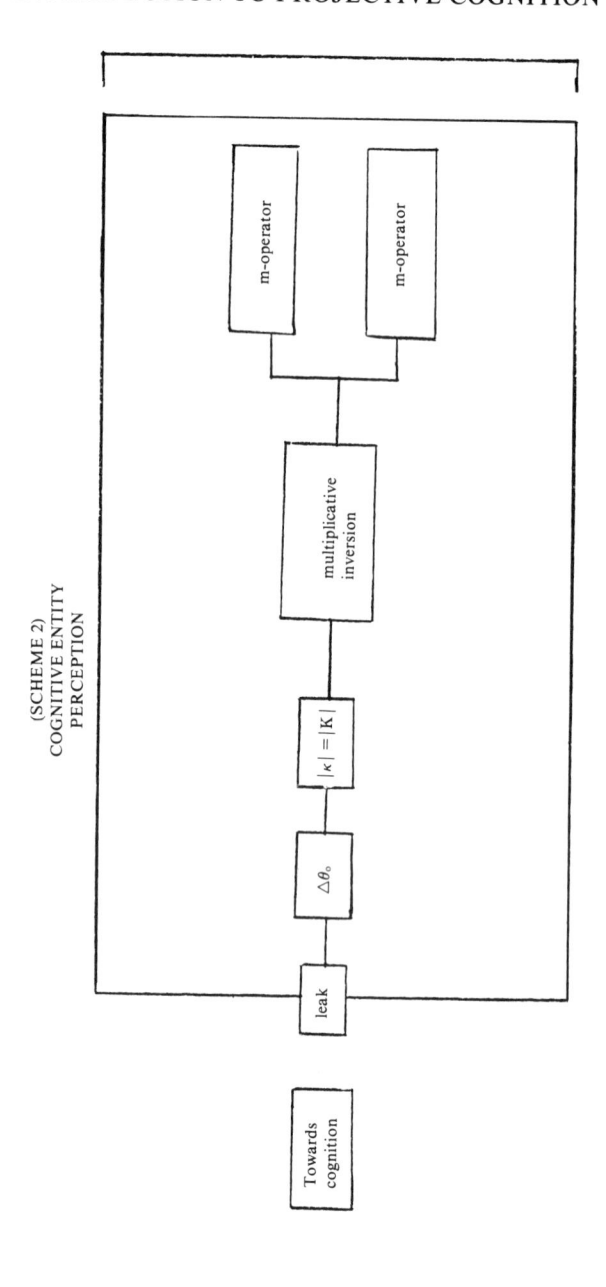

(SCHEME 2)
COGNITIVE ENTITY
PERCEPTION

m-operator

m-operator

multiplicative inversion

$|\kappa| = |K|$

$\Delta\theta_\circ$

leak

Towards cognition

Table #1

Geometrical Observations from Intuitional Perception

Equations: Advance per Revolution

Path	r^*	$\triangle\theta_{o1}$ (sec. of arc/rev.)	$\triangle\theta_{o2}$ (sec. of arc/rev.)
(1)	5.79×10^{12}	.45885	.10559
(2)	1.082×10^{13}	.33565	.07724
(3)	1.496×10^{13}	.28546	.06569
(4)	2.28×10^{13}	.23123	.05321

*r in cognitive unit

Table #2

Advance of Perihelia of Planets per Century
according to Intuitional Perception Equations

Orbit	r^*	$\triangle\theta_{o1}$ (sec. of arc/cent.)	$\triangle\theta_{o2}$ (sec. of arc/cent.)
Mercury	5.79×10^{12}	190.39	43.81
Venus	1.082×10^{13}	54.57	12.56
Earth	1.496×10^{13}	28.54	6.56
Mars	2.28×10^{13}	12.29	2.83

*r measured in centimeters.

100 INTRODUCTION TO PROJECTIVE COGNITION

TABLE #3

Deflection of a Ray of Light at Rim of Sun
Surface according to Intuitional Perception Equations.*

Unit	$\triangle \theta_{o_2}$ (radians)	$\triangle \theta_{o_2}$ (sec. of arc)
$q = \pi$	8.27618×10^{-6}	1.7070
$q = 1$	4.66933×10^{-6}	.96311

* r in cm

And q, in order to be one, has to deal with infinities (as cognition was defined previously in the sixth cognitive proposition).

The path of a ray of light would "suffer" a non-Euclidean perceptive deflection of 1.70 sec. of arc at a cognitive unit of $q = \pi$, and a non-Euclidean perceptive deflection of .96 sec. of arc at a cognitive unit of $q = 1$. A ray of light "straightens out" as it disappears cognitively into perception, that is, an undetermined cognitive unitary factor diminishes from $q = \pi$ to $q = 1$.

Fifth phenomenal proposition. The extension of linearity is a function of a non-Euclidean π expression.

From Equations #67 and Tables #1 and #2 we have

Sixth phenomenal proposition. If the *circle* in phenomena has $2\pi_p$ radians and the cognitive circle has $2\pi_c$ radians, then

Equation #69

$$2\pi_p^r \pm \triangle \theta_{o_2} = 2\pi_c^r$$

Intuitively, this is an Angular Equivalence relation. A perceptive leak can be obtained here by virtue of Equation #46. Equation #69 is in agreement with the corollary to the fourth cognitive proposition where $f(x)$ is equal to phenomena and $f(-x)$ is equal to phenomenon.

Then, the phenomenal world can be named Euclidean, the cognitive world Euclidean, and they are related by a non-Euclidean factor inherent in the human mind, evident through intuitive perception only.

When considering the R-C tensor as a perceptive-phenomenal link, if $|\kappa| = 0$, then $|K| = 0$ and $\triangle\theta_{o_2} = 0$ and

Equation #70

$$2\pi_p^r = 2\pi_c^r$$

Here, all alternatives are Euclidean. This suggests cognitive conclusions that *at all times* appear to be obvious. Then

Seventh phenomenal proposition. All cognitions can not be taken as exact phenomenal happenings.

That is, not all that we "see" is really happening in the phenomenal world.

Cosmological Perceptive Principles

Finally, then, if Q is equal to phenomenal projection and Q' is equal to perceptive projection we have that, in general

Equation #71

$$Q = Q' \pm A$$

where A is equal to $\triangle\theta_{o_2}$.

Eighth phenomenal proposition. Every perception associated with a surface of revolution will produce a continuous deformation into itself in such a way that each path associated with $|K|$ crosses over itself.

Corollary. If $|\kappa|$ is associated with phenomena (Cv) and $|K|$ is associated with perception (Cv₁) then $|\kappa| = |K|$ constitutes a necessary and sufficient condition for a path to be a part of a perceptive surface of revolution.

Ninth phenomenal proposition. Of all cognitive properties associated with a surface of revolution there is at least *one* of a perceptive nature.

Symbolic Summary of Chapter Seven

The reader is referred to page 6, Chapter 1, for the symbolic definitions.

1) Dirac: belongs to Cs where x = 1.

2) Imagination and Intuition: They belong to OCs or OCv_1 where x = −1 and x = 2 respectively.

3) R-C tensor: Here Cv progresses into OCv_1. And $|\kappa|$ will result. It might "leak" out as Cv progressing into OCv_2.

4) $d = \dfrac{K}{\pi}$: Here Cv_2 progresses into OCv_2. And $|K|$ will result.

5) $\dfrac{1}{2} re^{-\epsilon} \epsilon^1$: Here Cv progresses into OCv_1.

6) λ: a) 0^- (operator) progresses into Cs. It occurs in other than human species. b) 0^- (operator) progresses into "nothing" or Cv progresses into OCv_1. In this alternative a "leak" might occur as Cv progressing into OCv_2 (as in the advance of the perihelion of Mercury, the bending of a ray of light at the surface of the sun, or the parallel line paradox).

7) $|\kappa| = |K|$: OCv_1 is identified with OCv_2 purposely.

8) Table #1: This is the result of OCv_2 progressing into Cs. Here we have a definition of point geometry as equivalent to positionality.

9) Table #2: This is the result of OCv_2 progressing into OCs.

10) Equation #69: Here OCv_1 progresses purposely into OCv_2 but then it might "leak" out into Cs as in the advance of the perihelion of Mercury.

Equation #72

a) No orbital change (no "leak")

$2\pi_c^r$ = blank (no awareness)

$2\pi_p^r$ = blank (absolute nothingness)

b) Orbital change ("leak")

$2\pi_c^r \pm \triangle\theta_{o_2} \cong$ blank (cognitive observer)

$2\pi_p^r \pm \triangle\theta_{o_2} \cong$ blank (phenomenal entity)

11) Examples of $|\kappa| = |K|$ on purpose events:
    a) Bending of a ray of light at the periphery of the sun surface. Here, the calculated OCs progresses into OC_{V_1}.
    b) Parallel line paradox: Here OC_{V_1} progresses into OCs.

Perceptive Orbital Motion

As *r* varies, a perceptive fourth dimension within *r* (not time) is formed, created within the framework of the cognitive three-dimensional world.

If x approaches infinity (comes close to positional phenomenality) Equation #53 (the R-C tensor) approaches 0 and we have Euclidean dimensions. But if x approaches infinity as *r* approaches one point, we have $\triangle\theta_{o_2} = \frac{1}{\sqrt{\pi}}$, a limit in this fourth (perceptual) dimension.

At *r* equal to cognitive infinity (x is equal to one), $\triangle\theta_{o_2} = 0$ and the two "Euclidean" worlds would coincide. Whatever the word "Universe" means can be perceived by anyone able to "see" a fourth dimension, as sketched out of a three-dimensional expression.

Several questions arise that cannot be ignored. For example, why the selective leaks of perceptions (the arbitrary appearance of Equation #46 might explain this) that should have remained "unconscious" appear in the cognitive world? Here we have the advance of the perihelia of the different planets and the bending of a ray of light at the rim of the sun surface. Certainly there is no leak in surfaces of revolution where the *point geometry* is reduced to dimensions within the scope of the senses; we see no "advance" of a point in the locus of a circle in constant revolution at everyday cognitive velocities. Here, at a small r (r equal to a small cognitive unit) $\Delta\theta_{o_2}$ would produce a perceptive advance of approximately one radian! And why do we obtain a greater increase in $\Delta\theta_{o_2}$ in a supposedly lower species if imagination is assumed to exist in them? And what about the world of atoms and electrons? The smallest orbit of the hydrogen atom would show an approximate advance of 9.7×10^5 degrees per revolution! Here, if we consider part b) of Equation #72 and assume ourselves to be a phenomenal entity, then

Equation #73

One cognitive revolution/rev $\approx \dfrac{\Delta\theta_{o_2}}{2\pi_c^2}$ perceptive revolutions/rev

If the radius for the smallest orbit of hydrogen is equal to 5.29×10^{-9} cm and the velocity of an electron for this orbit is 2.2×10^8 cm/sec and this velocity value is arbitrarily assumed to be a perceptive measure (by virtue of the ninth phenomenal proposition) then the cognitive velocity of the electron would be reduced, by Equation #73, to the order of 10^4 cm/sec (8.16×10^4 cm/sec) or .816 Km/sec. This might represent a Newtonian planetary-like phenomenal system almost similar to our cognitive planetary system.

Certainly, the few intuitive perceptions that we have witnessed cannot be the only ones to exist between phenomena and cognition. There should be more, and only a special intuitive mind could feel their significance.

One would hope that these occasional perceptions fall into an evolutionary pattern that make them more frequent as the human brain evolves towards a more realistic union with true phenomena. One might be tempted to think that man is destined to better things after he finally leaves behind common actual cognition.

Fortunately, the analysis of our initial spherical system can be oriented in the following way: if part b), Equation #72, is considered from a perceptive point of view, then

Equation #73(a)

One perceptive revolution/rev. $\approx \dfrac{2\pi_C^r}{\Delta \theta_{o_2}}$ cognitive revolutions/rev.

Next, let us consider the *cognitive angular velocity* of the sun $\left(\dfrac{d\theta}{dT}\right)_c$ and calculate the *perceptive angular velocity* of the sun $\left(\dfrac{d\theta}{dT}\right)_p$ Making use of Equation #73 and Equation #67

Equation #74

$$\left(\dfrac{d\theta}{dT}\right)_p = \dfrac{1}{2\pi_C^r} \left[\dfrac{e^B}{\sqrt{(\pi |a|)}}\right]^{rad} \left(\dfrac{d\theta}{dT}\right)_c$$

The rotational cognitive angular momentum of the sun is $\dfrac{2}{5} M R^2 \cdot \left(\dfrac{d\theta}{dT}\right)_c \approx 10^{42}$ kg-meters^2-sec^{-1} where R is equal to *a* and measured in meters and M is measured in kilograms. From this datum $\left(\dfrac{d\theta}{dT}\right)_c$ is found to be approximately equal to 2.6×10^{-6} rad./sec. Substituting this value in Equation #74 we find that $\left(\dfrac{d\theta}{dT}\right)_p$ is approximately equal to 1.9×10^{-11} rad/sec. Using this last result, the perceptive angular momentum of the sun would amount to $\dfrac{2}{5} M R^2 \left(\dfrac{d\theta}{dT}\right)_p \approx 7.43 \times 10^{36}$ kg-meters^2-sec^{-1}.

If for the planets, *a* is the semi-major axis, then

Equation #75

$$V_c = a \left(\frac{d\theta}{dT}\right)_c$$

where V_c is an approximation of the orbital velocity in our present system. Since

Equation #76

$$V_c = \frac{2\pi a}{P}$$

is also a good approximation, then

Equation #77

$$\left(\frac{d\theta}{dT}\right)_c = \frac{2\pi}{P}$$

where P is the orbital period. Equation #74 can be expressed as

Equation #78

$$\left(\frac{d\theta}{dT}\right)_p = \frac{e^B}{\sqrt{\pi}} \left(\frac{|a|^{-\frac{1}{2}}}{P}\right)$$

the *perceptive angular velocity* of the planets in our new perceptive system.

If we proceed to determine the *perceptive angular momentum* of the planets in this system with the cognitive radius a and mass m of each planet, then

Equation #79

$$L = ma^2 \left(\frac{d\theta}{dT}\right)_p \quad \text{kg-meters}^2\text{-sec}^{-1}$$

represents the perceptive angular momentum L of each planet in our perceptive system. If in Equation #79 we substitute $\left(\frac{d\theta}{dT}\right)_p$ as already expressed in Equation #78 we would have

Equation #80

$$L = \frac{me^B |a|^{1.5}}{\sqrt{\pi P}} \text{ kg-meters}^2\text{-sec}^{-1}$$

for each planet, where $|a|^{1.5}$ meters^2 is equal to $|a|^{-.5}|a|^2$ meters^2.

The total sum for the perceptive angular momentum of the planets would be 6.03×10^{36} kg-meters^2-sec^{-1}. This means that, in this system, the sun accounts for 55.18% of the total angular momentum and the planets for 44.82% of the total angular momentum.

Equation #80 can be simplified as follows,

Equation #81

$$P = \frac{me^B |a|^{1.5}}{\sqrt{\pi L}}$$

and if

Equation #82

$$\sqrt{p} = \frac{me^B}{\sqrt{\pi L}} = \text{constant}$$

then

Equation #83

$$P^2 = .p |a|^3$$

this being a qualified version equivalent to Kepler's third law of planetary motion.

The centripetal force in this perceptive system would be

Equation #84

$$F_p = ma\left(\frac{d\theta}{dT}\right)^2_p$$

108 INTRODUCTION TO PROJECTIVE COGNITION

Making use of Equation #78 and Equation #83, Equation #84 can be expressed as

Equation #85

$$F_p = \frac{me^{2B}}{\pi pa^3}$$

where the absolute value for *a* is dropped since the unit meter is reduced to the third power. This last Equation defines the centripetal perceptive force of the orbit. Since

$$p = \frac{m^2 e^{2B}}{\pi L^2}$$

Equation #85 reduces to

Equation #86

$$F_p = \frac{L^2}{ma^3}$$

a well-known relation for circular orbits. From the above results, the following findings can be stated: a) The atomic world might be reduced to a Newtonian-like system by means of the perceptive formulas, b) Kepler's third law of planetary motion retains its equivalence in its perceptive journey towards cognition (although the constants are different), c) the phenomenal-cognitive less solid principle stated earlier is valid concerning the total angular momentum and centripetal forces in our planetary system.

If, as in Classical mechanics, we assume that the mutual gravitational force between two bodies is proportional to the product of the two masses (and this is a *linear* relation by Newton's third law of motion, therefore perceptively valid), then by using Equation #85

Equation #87

$$\frac{me^{2B}}{\pi pa^3} = \frac{G_p mM}{a^3} = F_{p.\ grav.}$$

if Equation #83 is to be sustained.

This Equation defines the perceptive gravitational force between two bodies. Then

Equation #88

$$\frac{e^{2B}}{\pi p} = G_p M$$

where G_p is the perceptive gravitational constant. Substituting Equation #82 in Equation #88 we obtain,

Equation #89

$$G_p = \frac{L^2}{m^2 M}$$

Making use of Equation #80 we finally obtain

Equation #90

$$G_p = \frac{e^{2B}|a|^3}{\pi M P^2}$$

remembering the note on the units of $|a|^3$ (meters^4) mentioned in Equation #80. This results in an approximate G_p value equal to 2.56×10^{-9} cm^4-gm^{-1}-seg^{-2}. This last Equation establishes an unequalified perceptive version of Kepler's third law of motion

Nothing new has been obtained here that is different in formulation from Newtonian mechanics. Only the results, brought about by the value of p (Equation #82), have been altered. And these results are perceptive, unconscious data that invariably generate the cognitive Newtonian world.

Thus, the following principles seem to be general in our *perceptive* orbital system:

1) The planetary orbits are compatible with circular configuration, with the cognitive semi-major axis as the radius.

2) Cognitive rates of change are bound to perceptive modification.

3) The mutual perceptive force between two bodies is inversely proportional to the cube of the distance between them.

It might be said that the perceptive values obtained are the *truth* in the nature of things while the cognitive values are meaningful realities in the constitution of the human mind. Both are essentially valid and determine a unique *dual* state that allow the existence of a twin, parallel world.

Appendix

It is interesting to note that a second solution to Equation #56 that satisfies Equation #57 in the text could be

Equation #1

$$\left(|\kappa|\, r\right)^{-1/x} = e^{\frac{1}{2f(x)}}$$

that yields, following the same mathematical process used in Chapter Seven to obtain other than human results [$f(x) = x = 1$],

Equation #2

$$(\text{Con})(\text{Im}) = |\kappa|^\circ = 1$$

and

Equation #3

$$(\text{Im})(\text{In}) = |\kappa|^{1/2} = r^{-1/2}\, e^{-.25}$$

Equation #2, as stated here, defines nature (phenomena) by itself.

Since no human cognitive or perceptive process exists in the establishment of nature by herself, the human alternative $f(x) = e^x$ does not belong here. Hence, it is proposed that

Equation #4

a) $0*0 = f(\tau,\Sigma) = 1$

b) $0_1*0_1 = \Sigma^{-\frac{1}{2}} e^{-.25} = |\kappa|^{\frac{1}{2}}$

where $0*, 0*_1$ and $0, 0_1$ are unreal operators, defines *pure phenomenal expressions* that belong in nature by herself.

Bibliography

Alvarez Villar, A. *Elementos de Psicología Experimental*. Madrid: Aguilar S.A. De Ediciones, 1966.

Beiser, Authur. *Conceptos de Física Moderna*. New York: McGraw Hill Book Co. Inc., 1963.

Berkeley, George. *A Treatise Concerning The Principles of Human Knowledge*. New York: Dolphin Books.

Bochenski, J.M. *Introducción al Pensamiento Filosófico*. Barcelona: Editorial Herder, 1973. Trans. by Daniel Ruiz Bueno.

Delacre, George. *El Tiempo en Perspectiva*. San Juan: Editorial Universitaria, Universidad de Puerto Rico, 1975.

Einstein and others. *The Principle of Relativity*. New York: Dover Publications, Inc., 1923.

Eisenhart, L.P. *Differential Geometry*. Boston: Ginn and Company, 1937.

Fatone, Vicente. *Lógica e Introducción a la Filosofía*. Buenos Aires: Editorial Kapelusz, 1951.

Freud, Sigmund. *An Outline of Psychoanalysis*. New York: W.W. Norton & Co., Inc., 1940.

Gemignani, Michael C. *Basic Concepts of Mathematics and Logic*. Addison-Wesley Publishing Co., Inc., 1968.

Guttinger, W. *Generalized Functions and Disperse Relations in Physics.* Fortschritte der Physik 14, 483-602 (1966).

Hartmann, Nicolai. *Metafísica del Conocimiento.* Buenos Aires: Editorial Lozada, S.A., 1957. Trans. by J. Rovira Armengol.

Heidegger, Martin. *Discourse on Thinking.* New York: Harper Colophon Books, Harper & Row, 1966. Trans. by John M. Anderson and Hans Freund.

Howe, Michael J.A. *Introduction to Human Memory—A Psychological Approach.* New York: Harper & Row, 1970.

Hume, David. *An Enquiry Concerning Human Understanding.* New York: Dolphin Books.

Husserl, Edmund. *Ideas.* New York: Collier Books, Fourth Printing, 1972. Trans. by W.R. Boyce Wilson.

The Phenomenology of Internal Time Consciousness. Bloomington, Ind.: Indiana University Press, 1964.

Cartesian Meditations. The Hague, Netherlands: Martinus Nijhoff, 1973.

Jolivet, Regis. *Tratado de Filosofía, Lógica y Cosmología.* Buenos Aires: Ediciones Carlos Lohle, 1960.

Kant, Immanuel. *Crítica de la Razón Pura.* Buenos Aires: Editorial Lozada, S.A., Seventh edition, 1973. Trans. by Jose del Perojo.

Kaplan, Irving. *Nuclear Physics.* Reading, Mass.: Addison-Wesley Publishing Co., Inc., 1964.

Kaplan, Wilfred. *Advanced Calculus.* Reading, Mass.: Addison-Wesley Publishing Co., Inc., 1952.

Knopp, Konrad. *Elements of the Theory of Functions.* New York: Dover Publications, Inc., 1952.

Locke, John. *An Essay Concerning Human Understanding.* New York: Doubleday & Co., Inc., 1961. Abridged by Richard Taylor.

Menzel, Donald H. *Mathematical Physics.* New York: Dover Publications, Inc., 1961.

Merleau-Ponty, M. *Phenomenology of Perception.* London: Routledge and Kegan Paul., 1962. Trans. by Colin Smith.

Messiah, Albert. *Quantum Mechanics.* Amsterdam: North-Holland Publishing Co., 1962. Trans. by G.M. Temmer.

Mira y Lopez, Emilio. *El Pensamiento.* Buenos Aires: Editorial Kapelusz, S.A., 1966.

Bibliography 115

Neisser, Ulric. *Cognitive Psychology*. New York: Meredith Publishing Co., 1967.

Planck, Max. *A Survey of Physical Theory*. New York: Dover Publications, Inc., 1960.

Rainich, G.Y. *Mathematics of Relativity*. New York: John Wiley & Sons, Inc., 1950.

Romero, Francisco. *Lógica e Introducción a la Problemática Filosófica*. Buenos Aires: Editorial Lozada, S.A., 1973.

Sartre, Jean-Paul. *Lo Imaginario*. Buenos Aires: Editorial Lozada, S.A., 1964. Trans. by Manuel Lamana.

Schiff, Leonard I. *Quantum Mechanics*. New York: McGraw-Hill Book Co., Inc., Third Edition, 1968.

Schwarts, Jacob T. *Introduction to Matrices and Vectors*. New York: McGraw-Hill Book Co., Inc., 1961.

Smith and Jacobs. *Introductory Astronomy and Astrophysics*. Philadelphia: W.B. Saunders Co., 1973.

Sommerville, D.M.Y. *Elements of Non-Euclidean Geometry*. New York: Dover Publications, Inc., 1958.

Spain, Barry. *Tensor Calculus*. Edinburgh and London: Oliver and Boyd, 1953.

Synge, J.L. *Relativity: The General Theory*. Amsterdam: North-Holland Publishing Co., 1966.

Torreti, Roberto. *Manuel Kant*. Santiago, Chile: Ediciones de la Universidad de Chile, 1967.

Weyl, Hermann. *Space, Time, Matter*. New York: Dover Publications, Inc., 1922.

Wills, A.P. *Vector Analysis with an Introduction to Tensor Analysis*. New York: Dover Publications, Inc., 1958.

Woodsworth & Schlosberg. *Experimental Psychology*. New York: Holt, Rinehart and Winston, 1954.